What Peopl
The Rumble Zone

"Based upon his 20+ years as an executive coach and workshop facilitator, Jim Boneau has captured the quintessence of what it really takes to grow and succeed as a leader. Stop overthinking things, let go of old judgments, and summon the courage to rumble. Embrace the chaos, the disharmony of life and the barbs of onlookers. A determined mindset is important to achieve greatness, but equally important is learning how to surface discordant narratives without allowing them to discourage. *The Rumble Zone* is a playbook for seeking the types of development situations that make us all better leaders, spouses, parents and humans.

From the opening pages of this important work, we are reminded that great leaders and personal achievement often spring from disharmony and conflict. Boneau encourages the reader and practitioner to courageously embrace the rumble and those uncomfortable group dynamics that so often stimulate us to greatness. This is a must read for anyone looking to be reminded that the best opportunities for professional development are discovered in the times of greatest change and conflict."

–John DiLullo, CEO, LastLine

"*The Rumble Zone. Leadership Strategies In The Rough & Tumble Of Change* could not be more a relevant and timely message. And Jim is the one to deliver it! From surviving cancer, to living his own authenticity as a gay man, to his extensive 30-plus-years' career advancing senior level leaders internationally, Jim lives inside a rumble of complexity, ambiguity, uncertainty and change. Read this important book and take heart: you can learn to live and thrive inside the rumble of our rapidly-changing world!"

–Susanne Biro, Coach to C-suite and executive level leaders. *Forbes* and *CEO Magazine* contributing writer.

"Add to Jim Boneau's titles of master-teacher, master-facilitator, and master-coach – master-author. You will be drawn in by Jim's true, vulnerable, authentic, evocative stories and will learn a valuable life lesson as a result of each. The reflection activities at the end of each chapter personalize and activate Jim's powerful words. This book is a must read, not just for leaders, but for anyone wanting to live more in the present, more authentic, more capable, and happier lives, especially in times of chaos and change."

–Bill Gardner, Managing Partner, Noetic Outcome

"*The Rumble Zone* is a MUST READ for anyone leading, facilitating or experiencing change. Through masterful storytelling and real case studies, Jim [the author] approaches his subject from a unique perspective. The result is pure triumph at a time when it's needed more than ever. BRAVO!"

–Rebecca Nelson, Chief Learning Officer Corning, Inc.

"In *The Rumble Zone*, I have been inspired by Jim's courage in sharing his own vulnerabilities, limitations and challenges as illustrations of a pathway for his own growth. This is the courage of a true leader - to go 'there' openly and honestly and create a path that others can follow. And what a helpful path! The coherence of the process shines through: reading this is like sitting with a wise, non-judgmental mentor helping to process life's challenges. Jim's clarity in articulating the 9 components of the Rumble Zone have made it much more straightforward for me to see where the gaps are in my own skill-set for coping with change. Highly recommended!"

–Dr. Jane Bentley, Music and Wellbeing Specialist

"*The Rumble Zone* will force you to face challenges from a new perspective. Personal at times, provoking at times, always constant in message. This is a book every leader should have on their desk. Jim Boneau provides the framework to face and grow from the constant change every organization and every leader faces today."

-James Flowers, General Sales Manager/Financial Services Director, Power Ford.

"*The Rumble Zone* is so much more than a book about leadership. It's a manual of useful strategies to navigate the world, not only in business, but also in life. The experiences Mr. Boneau shares are valuable and surprisingly personal. He opens his life and allows the reader into his world. In so doing, he captures the reader and keeps them engrossed. He encourages all of us to take on the rumble…to take on life as it comes."

–Tess St John, Author

"Beautifully crafted storytelling with leadership wisdom that is as relevant as it is thoughtful and transformational. Jim Boneau brings us into his world as a drum circle and leadership development facilitator and we feel the beat and the rhythm as he invites us to rumble in our own lives. His stories are real and raw, and they entertain while teaching critical lessons around leadership and life."

–Geoff Scales, President, Dialogik Creative Leadership Inc.

"To rumble in rhythm is to shake yourself forward and land in a leap of faith groove that grows the self, community, and company to new levels of aliveness."

–Christine Stevens, Founder, UpBeat Drum Circles, Author, Speaker, Poet

"Shine new light and perspective on the challenges unique to *your* life through Jim's story of Emotional Intelligence applied. Just as the humble Wizard of Oz revealed, these tools (or gifts) reside within, and are yours for the asking."

–John Hayden, Entrepreneur, Founder of JAMTOWN

"I didn't quite believe Jim Boneau's story in the first chapter, about how a group of people – non-drummers – could come together and make music. I could feel my own resistance to the trust Jim put in, as the facilitator, to allow the group to make it through a rumble successfully. Now I'm convinced – the rumble metaphor is perfect for what we go through in life, and the trust it takes to walk into them with courage and come out with beautiful music. In his book, Jim has shed a light on our personal rumbles and how to navigate them with empathy, compassion and effectiveness. I found many ways to help myself through my own challenges, being present, saying what needs said and building resilience. But I learned the most from the personal stories he shares, which have a vulnerability that truly deepens the experience of this read as well as the lesson it ties to – I was touched by his candor and felt myself seeing my own stories. This is a book that will make you think, think deeply about who you are and who you want to be - then it compels you to act. I highly recommend The Rumble Zone to anyone who wants to walk through their challenges with more success and more grace."

–Stacey Sargent, CEO, Connect Growth and Development

"The simplicity of the rumble concept is deceiving, as it takes commitment, patience, courage, vulnerability, and faith to allow ourselves to identify and embrace the path of an often uncomfortable, yet ultimately gratifying, rumble. I have had the blessing of working with Jim for several years and he remains one of the most impactful people in my life. In this book, he walks us through his own rumble journeys with a steady hand while coaching us with confidence and vision. This book is like sitting down on the couch and having a real, raw conversation with Jim. You'll leave inspired by his challenges, humility, and wisdom to embrace the discomfort and the uncertainty in your own life. This book will provoke your thoughts about that path you've only dared to dream about but, if you truly open yourself up to the rumble inside, you'll have the power and will to pursue."

–Lisa Stephens, Leadership Development Specialist

"Reading this book was like having Jim sat right next to me telling his story; Jim is probably the most inspirational person that I have ever had the pleasure to work with and learn from and I'm now lucky enough to call him a friend; no-one does authenticity and generosity like Jim Boneau and this book is just that – a gift from the heart to help others navigate this crazy world in which we live!"

–Coralie Hooper, Leadership Development Master Facilitator & Coach

"The author masterfully and courageously shares his life rumbles with the reader and, at the same time, provides expert instruction to them on how to navigate their own rumbles. I, for one, am glad the author listened to the 'angel in a tow truck wearing overalls' and followed his dreams. His clients are lucky to be able to learn from his wisdom and expertise."

–Stacy Duhon, Stacy Duhon Coaching

"In *The Rumble Zone*, Jim Boneau guides us to the gifts that lie in The Rumble Zone — 'the place between what once was and what is emerging.'

Jim's stories from the Rumble Zone show how natural and accessible his eight strategies really are — though they require us to "do something different" than what is familiar or comfortable. That "something different" usually has to do with seeing and acknowledging reality at a deeper level. Jim gives us tools to reach for those deeper understandings of ourselves, others, and the situation, so that we can respond from our strongest, most integrated self.

The element that really sets Jim's story apart is his framing of "Rumble" — uncertainty or transition — from the viewpoint of group music-making, or drum circles. In this perspective, we can see Rumbles as natural waves. They rise, disrupt the old, present opportunities for new. Our choices in the midst of them determine what happens next.

Now we are all plunged into the biggest Rumble of our lives, the coronavirus pandemic. Faced with more uncertainty than we ever thought possible, we must draw on our inner resources more than ever. *The Rumble Zone* is a timely guide providing focus and reassurance to help us find greater discernment, empathy, and courage to chart our course through turbulent times. It's a source of clarity and hope for me."

–Mary Tolena, Organizational Consultant and Entrepreneur

"The book put a name - rumble - to something that I've experienced but could never put into words. 'Inflection point' or similar doesn't capture the messy, ambiguous, exhilarating, emotional nature of such experiences."

–Colin Bodell, Vice President of Engineering, Shopify Plus

THE RUMBLE ZONE

LEADERSHIP STRATEGIES

IN THE
ROUGH & TUMBLE
OF
CHANGE

JIM BONEAU

Copyright © 2020, Jim Boneau

All rights reserved. No part of this book may be used or reproduced by any means, graphic, electronic, or mechanical (including any information storage retrieval system) without the express written permission from the author, except in the case of brief quotations for use in articles and reviews wherein appropriate attribution of the source is made.

Published in the United States by Ignite Press.
www.ignitepress.us/

ISBN: 978-1-950710-43-0 (Amazon Print)
ISBN: 978-1-950710-44-7 (IngramSpark) PAPERBACK
ISBN: 978-1-950710-45-4 (IngramSpark) HARDCOVER
ISBN: 978-1-950710-46-1 (Smashwords)

For bulk purchase and for booking, contact:

Jim Boneau
jim@therumblegroup.com
www.therumblezone.com

Because of the dynamic nature of the Internet, web addresses or links contained in this book may have been changed since publication and may no longer be valid. The content of this book and all expressed opinions are those of the author and do not reflect the publisher or the publishing team.
The author is solely responsible for all content included herein.

This book is dedicated to my mom, Ann Boneau.
The greatest example in my life of a leader who led
from the heart.

Acknowledgements

> Let gratitude be the pillow upon which you kneel to say your nightly prayer.
>
> –Maya Angelou

This book is possible, in large part, because of the communities of friends, colleagues, clients and family who have supported and included me throughout the years. And within each of those communities, there are specific individuals to whom I am incredibly grateful for their individual contribution to my life and this work.

Arthur Hull started as my teacher, invited me as a training partner and is the person with whom I have collaborated professionally longer than anyone else. For 20 years, Arthur has generously shared his wisdom, accepted my coaching, and inspired me to find my unique voice. Together, we found the connections between community drum circle facilitation, leadership development and personal growth. We taught workshops around the world, ignited human potential, nurtured communities, and had a lot of fun in the process. So much of the work in this book references and extends his teachings. He built a platform and gave me space to stand with him. Arthur's platform was built in part by his teachers, and to thank Arthur is also to thank his teachers. I never met Babatunde Olatunji, but I know I'm grateful to Baba; not only for his influence with Arthur, but his influence on culture and music. Baba was one of the early African teachers who introduced drumming and rhythms to the US. The spirit of the drum is part of the heart of this book. I acknowledge the drum, the rhythms and the teachers who inspired our modern-day drum circles.

I wouldn't be a part of this drum community without Cameron Tummel's invitation to my first Hawaii Playshop. I wouldn't have stayed at that first playshop without the efforts of those who reached out to me early on: Ken, Lulu, Susan, and Don. Mary Tolena, you saw in me possibilities that I did not see in myself. Early on, you encouraged me to share my voice in ways I only dreamed of. Your partnership is invaluable to me. Also, at that first Playshop, I met John Hayden, who would bridge from drummer community to Seattle family.

My Seattle family has become my everyday lifeblood. That would not have happened, had John Hayden not invited me to Seattle to attend a festival, two weeks after that first Hawaii Playshop. John Hayden is a brother, a friend, and a companion in many of the most impactful and influential stories in this book – which are the stories of my life. There really are no words I can write to express the full extent of the acknowledgement and appreciation I have for John. And, I know he knows. It was John who introduced me to the core of my Seattle family. If John is one foundation of this family, Stacia is the other. Thank you Stacia for your love, acceptance and encouragement to be me. Thank you for your selflessness in reflecting back to me who you saw; a man struggling to accept who he really was. You turned a situation that could have been full of bitterness and anger into one of learning, loving and acceptance. MJ, Vickie, Christy, Jack, Jane, Skye, Lily, Emma and Wendulien – Seattle would not be the same without you, my Seattle family.

I am forever grateful for the education, experiences and friends I met pursuing my master's degree at the Leadership Institute of Seattle. My teachers, Cheryl & Pam, my systems counselors, Clancy and Mark, the members of my academic track, Stacey, Susanne and Stacy and my study group, Stacey, PJ, Robert, and Barbara– all of you were key for me, making the most of all those long sessions, intense I-Groups and seemingly impossible hurdles to cross. Some of you became much more than colleagues. You became part of my everyday life. Stacey, your friendship and professionalism inspire me. Stacy, your coaching helped me start this book. PJ, your total acceptance of me is a gift in my life. Susanne, you called me to action by introducing me to the springboard for my professional career as a leadership development practitioner, Bluepoint.

Thank you to the Bluepoint community for providing me the opportunities to coach and facilitate across the world. Gregg, Bryn, David, Joan, Lisa, Brian, Ashley, Geoff, Bill, Lisa and all the administrative staff, coaches and facilitators who embraced me as a leader, thank you for teaching me through the work you do. Thank you to the clients who brought me into your organizations and trusted me with your leaders: Cherie, Rebecca, Rich, and the others who said 'Yes' to our unique leadership development approach. And to all those who attended my workshops and trusted me as a coach; it's your courage and willingness to challenge yourselves that inspired me to keep doing this tough and rewarding work.

Influences came not just from my community in the US, but from abroad as well. Coralie Hooper, Paul Dear, Jane Bentley, Sunil Omanwar, Tomoko Yokota, Martina Weinberger, Eva Beasley, Cherie Gardiner and Bek Wermut all at some point hosted me internationally. You helped open my eyes to a world beyond my US roots.

Before drumming and Seattle, there was my life in Texas. I'm forever grateful to Rodney, Carl, Kathy, Kathy, Trish, Tamera and Melissa. Rodney and Carl were my first brothers away from my blood family. I'm sure I'm still storing something in your houses today. I'm storing a part of you in my heart.

Before Dallas, there was Groves. Growing up there, I found love and acceptance in the band community and St. Peter's Church. Tessy, Laura, Liz, Gloria, Robbie – you gave me such hope for a better tomorrow by inspiring me, as a young man, to be a leader. Mr. Almany and Mr. Wadenpfuhl, you were shining examples of what a teacher should be. Not only were you teachers, but you opened your family to me and included me as one of your own.

To my family, Mom, Mike, Dane, Karon, James, Katherine, Taylor, Mark and Amanda. We went through so much together. And we all found our way to the other side, on our own terms. Melvin, you were the father I needed as a young man and as an adult. I miss you. My mother taught me about servant leadership before I knew anything about it. You were a living example of what it means to be of service to the community. I am the person I am today because of you. I know that every day of my life.

And now, every day of my life, I am blessed and gifted with a partner who brings out the best in me, Eric Mowery. I love you, Eric. You seem to be the complement to every one of my shortcomings. Your strength continues to amaze me. Your love continues to humble me. Your willingness to hold down the house while I go off traveling week after week is something I am so grateful for. I couldn't do any of this without you.

Finally, thank you, Marcia Zina Mager. You believed I could write a book well before I believed it. Your wisdom and techniques helped me turn the blank pages into the book I've always wanted to write. You adapted to my needs, opened new doorways and shaped me into the author I am today. And then, you eagerly took the next step from writing coach to writing partner. I'm forever grateful for every phone call, every edited page, every word of encouragement, every bit of research, and every word of challenge and support you offered. Your spirit is infused in these pages. Thank you for the introduction to Everett at Ignite Press. Everett, thank you for the solid partnership in bringing this book through its final phase and into the hands of our readers.

Table of Contents

Foreword: Arthur Hull 1

Chapter 1: Willing to Rumble...3

Chapter 2: Rally Courage 13

Chapter 3: Be Present 29

Chapter 4: Share Your Point of View 41

Chapter 5: Get Curious 57

Chapter 6: Strive for Empathy 73

Chapter 7: Bring an Open Mind 85

Chapter 8: Take Action 95

Chapter 9: Find Resilience 105

Chapter 10: Navigating the Rumble of the Moment...................................115

Resources 125

About the Author 129

Foreword

> Now, more than ever, we find ourselves seeking ways
> to build community with an intention to serve, to inspire
> and to reach beyond what separates us.
>
> –Diana Hull

To successfully step into a moment of "Transitional Leadership" in your business, personal or spiritual life, it helps to bring with you your courage, as well as all of your experiential knowledge. When you are consciously stepping into a transition point in your life, it also helps to bring with you the acknowledgment of your fears and the simple fact that there is a lot that you don't know.

We are all "Elders in Training." This statement is especially true if you are a leader, a teacher, or if you are responsible for facilitating a group process towards an end goal. The opportunity for learning never stops in life, no matter how good you get at what you do. Some of your biggest elder-in-training learning opportunities appear when faced with a challenge.

Being humbly and courageously curious while dealing with those "Rumbles" that come to you, is one of the countless myriad things that Jim Boneau has taught me during our twenty-year training partnership together.

As a young man, my fire-in-the-belly passion for "facilitating human potential through rhythm" drove me on a mission that always pushed me beyond my teaching competencies, as well as my levels of emotional intelligence. Thank God I have had people supporting and mentoring me along the way like Jim Boneau. With a parallel vision and passion,

Jim has helped guide me in pioneering and nurturing our international community of Village Music Circle Rhythm CareGivers that exists today.

In his book, "The Rumble Zone – Leadership Strategies in the Rough & Tumble of Change," Jim Boneau has successfully combined what seems to be oil and water. At first glance, the act of leading a group of people and facilitating an interactive rhythm event appear to live in different worlds. And yet, with the closer look that Jim gives us, he reveals the compelling universal parallels of group and personal change processes that these two worlds have to offer us.

By laying his trials and tribulations in life on the line as story metaphors, Jim reveals functioning universal elements that we can use in our personal lives to be more effective and authentic individuals and leaders. In each chapter of this book, Jim establishes a fundamental learning element that becomes a useful tool to help develop the personal sensibilities and curiosities needed to be an effective leader.

The understandings and learnings that Jim has presented to us in each progressive chapter become a platform for the next practical and applicable learning to come in the book.

I have known Jim Boneau for a good chunk of his life, and I know most of the stories that he uses in his book to educate us on how to be an authentic leader in a world of change. But, by reading his book, Jim has taught me how to use the learnings from the challenges that come at us in life, to be able to lead successfully from deep curiosity and a strong heart.

So, now that you have read this foreword to the end, I will tell you a little secret.

Even though the title of this book is, "The Rumble Zone – Leadership Strategies in the Rough & Tumble of Change," it could just as easily be "The Rumble Zone - Living an Authentic Life in the Rough & Tumble of Change."

Share your Spirit. Arthur Hull

Arthur Hull is the founder of Village Music Circles, author of 4 books, an internationally known speaker and teacher and the father of the modern-day rhythma-culture drum circle movement.

Chapter 1

Willing To Rumble

> At the heart of each of us, whatever the imperfections, exists a silent pulse of perfect rhythm which connects us to the universe.
>
> –George Leonard

I'm standing in the center of a giant, air-conditioned conference room, with floor-to-ceiling windows on one wall. Outside, it's an overcast Seattle morning. Inside, surrounding me in a massive circle, sit 350 Microsoft engineers, each holding some type of drum or percussion instrument: hand-carved djembes from Africa; congas from South America; a variety of Remo manufactured drums; plus shakers, wood blocks, and metal bells of all kinds. This is one of the largest corporate drum circles I've ever facilitated. Although my real job – the one that pays my mortgage – is as a leadership development coach, my role today is to lead a team-building rhythm session for these high potential employees.

The faces staring back at me represent cultures from around the world: Indian, Chinese, South American, European, and American; mostly millennials, but, as in so many tech companies these days, the men clearly outnumber the women.

The group has been drumming now for about 10 minutes. Hundreds of hands bouncing on the goat-skin heads of drums; dozens and dozens of wooden sticks striking bells; crashing waves of glass beads rattling in shakers; and thunderous beats producing sound waves that can be felt vibrating the floor. It's a sheer sensory onslaught. A wild, rhythmic orchestration, ranging from a cacophony of random booms to a rhythmical groove as melodic as a lullaby. Considering, thirty minutes ago, these engineers had never even touched a percussive instrument, they're progressing well, slowly transforming into an orchestral drumming ensemble.

I've stood in the middle of hundreds of drum circles, weathering the sensory experience, attempting to facilitate the potential of chaos into community. This extraordinary rhythm bath happens whether the event is a small circle of 10 elderly men and women at a retirement center or 1000 Parkinson caregivers, patients, and doctors drumming together at the World Parkinson's Congress. The differences in size and population require various levels of complexity to facilitate, but each is equally and unforgettably inspiring. Every population and every size of a drumming circle creates an original rhythmic sound that ignites and impacts everyone listening.

This group of engineers is clearly enjoying the experience so far - smiling and laughing, listening to the sounds all around them, and finding spaces in the rhythm to make their own beats.

All these booms, bangs, shakes and rattles, once connected, turn into rhythmic songs, known as grooves. Groups are usually happiest when they are in the groove, playing together in sync with a common pulse, but everyone improvising their own beat. Each participant always tries to find their unique contribution to that groove. My role, as the facilitator of any drum circle, is to help create an event with happy people drumming; to support the group in making the best music they possibly can, given their limited time and skill level. In the end, drumming together can be a powerfully transformative experience for individuals, as well as the group.

As I stand there, eyes closed, listening to the ensemble, I notice the inevitable. The connected rhythmical groove begins to wobble. It's hard to sustain an improvisational, rhythmical groove with 350 inexperienced drummers for a long time. Frankly, that's not really my goal. The groove always shifts, changes, and falters at some point. In my training as a drum circle facilitator, we learned to be prepared for this inevitable transition.

Recognizing the Emerging Change

The wobbling in the circle begins to grow. A few of the engineers' heads pop up. Moments before, they had been looking down, eyes half closed, enjoying the beat. Now another expression is emerging on many faces. Something is wrong. The rhythmic groove is beginning to falter. Some look helpless, afraid the groove might fall apart - 'a train wreck' in drum circle facilitator lingo. Many are now looking at me, assuming I will save them. Others stop drumming all together, unable to cope with the rising ambiguity the wobble is creating for the group. Still others continue to have their heads down, playing blissfully, unaware of the deteriorating rhythmic connection of the group.

This is a beautiful moment of both awareness by some, and total lack of awareness by others. This, like so many other observations from the circle, reminds me of situations I encounter with my coaching and leadership development clients. My role, however, is different here - right now, my responsibility is to help this group navigate their way from one good groove to the next without getting too roughed up in the rhythm train wreck that can occur in the space between those connected, rhythmical grooves.

But I'm not going to save them. Not yet. I want to wait. How far can the group go on wobbling before total chaos emerges? The longer the groove wobbles, the more opportunity to listen their way out of the wobble and get a steady rhythmic beat agreement on their own. If the intervention is too soon, they might not believe in themselves as much as a team needs to.

There are many tools I can use to facilitate the transition from one groove to another in a drum circle. A facilitator can slowly quiet the group until the music fades to silence. Or possibly, bring the group to an immediate and dramatic stop and experience the powerful moment when 350 people go from drumming to silence in 4 counts. Another option is to speed up the tempo of the rhythm beyond the group's ability to keep the same rhythm, to let it all almost completely fall apart and hope a new groove emerges.

However, in this instance I choose to proceed with another tool. I choose to rumble.

Embracing the Rumble

In the drum circle world, a rumble is a time when everyone plays as many notes as they possibly can on their instrument. It sounds like joyful, celebratory, and loud chaos. Rumbles can be used for many purposes: to build energy, to end a groove, to escape from a sequence of facilitation moves that aren't working, or to facilitate the transition from one groove to another. While not fully sure where this rumble would lead, my instinct tells me to trust the group, to trust the rhythms, and to trust the rumble.

From the middle of the circle, I shake my hands vigorously in the air, which they learned earlier as the hand signal for rumble. We shift from a faltering groove to a chaotic rumble where no one knows what's happening, not even me. The potential exists for us to use this chaotic time of rumble to transition from one good groove to another. It's a bit of a courageous act to take as a facilitator. Some of the drummers might get so carried away in the rumble that their ability to focus and hear the new groove emerging is unattainable. Some people want more structure, more instruction to get to a new groove. They want to be given a part to play. Some people's hands are tired, and they want a break. But I believe in the group. I believe in the rhythm. I believe in the rumble. The chaotic frenzy continues. My doubts begin to creep in: maybe it was a poor choice to rumble. My heart races even faster as my head begins to mentally leaf through pages of books I've read to think of another facilitation alternative. But, somewhere deep within the rumble, a new common pulse begins to take shape. My body begins to rock and bounce to a pulse more easily felt than heard. I'm willing to take action in the chaos to show the potential new beat. The question is, will the engineers be open-minded about the potential of the faltering groove and feel what's emerging?

> "*Rumble is the bridge between what once was and what is emerging. The more intentionally we walk that bridge, the more likely we are to create the environment for the best possible circumstances to emerge.*"

The look on the faces of many drummers during a rumble is one of pure joy. The energy feels like an explosive ending; a celebration, the exclamation point at the end of a wild outburst. But the faces of these engineers during this rumble offer a different expression: a steel-eyed sense of determination and commitment to get to another groove. They know how great it felt to be in the groove - and they want it back. They want another ride on the rhythmic wave and they know they have the capability to do it.

And then, we begin to hear it - the beginning of a new pulse that will shape our groove for the next 10 minutes. Before long, the group syncs up to this new beat. The joy in the room seems even more palpable than it was before, because now the group knows they can play a good groove, have it falter, and then find a new one. We have accessed another level of their potential as individuals and as a group.

Over the past 20 years, I've worked with thousands of executives across the globe as a leadership coach and workshop facilitator. My clients have been Fortune Top 10 organizations, tech-startups, and NGOs, which provided exposure to a broad set of global leaders. Repeatedly, I listened to leaders who were struggling through change. Often, those changes involved learning a new skill, adapting an old way of doing something, or partnering with new people. In each of these cases, they were being asked to shift from one way of doing something to another way of doing something. This level of change can create fear and ambiguity. In fact, that is often how my clients show up initially: emotional and anxious, wanting to move out of ambiguity and get into a new pattern. My coaching clients were, in fact, rumbling – trying to adjust to this unfamiliar, unknown, and often chaotic space that exists between old patterns and a new path waiting to emerge.

Most of us usually want relief from this place. We want to move away from the discomfort as soon as possible. We think of the time in between two good events as a time to get through as fast as possible, so we can feel relief. But, just like the rumble in a drum circle, this time of anxiety and ambiguity is a bridge. It's the inevitable place of feeling uncomfortable and full of self-doubt when learning a new skill. It's the place where we feel resistance to letting go of old judgements; that the new will never work. It's the mixed feelings of sadness and excitement, as we risk being vulnerable so we can connect to another.

I always encourage clients to embrace this discomfort, or at least acknowledge it. I challenge their assumptions, ask hard questions, "kick up dust" around them, purposely causing chaotic thoughts to emerge. And inevitably, one of those unexpected thoughts ends up launching a new relationship, career, or life path. I'm the facilitator calling in the rumble; strategically using that chaotic time to discover new insights, new possibilities, and new pathways.

Rumble is the bridge between what once was and what is emerging. The more intentionally we walk that bridge, the more likely we are to create the environment for the best possible circumstances to emerge. Yet, as human beings, we all resist change. But, no matter how hard we resist, the rumble is happening all around us, in every aspect of our lives. Personal and professional. I'm constantly navigating a state of rumble. Whether it's switching careers – leaving a secure corporate position to follow my dream of becoming a leadership coach; or my health – battling and surviving cancer; or relationships – finally coming out as a gay man – all of these challenging life situations required my willingness to rumble, over and over. Sometimes I can ride the changes easily because I'm less committed to what was, or more willing to try something new. Those are the rumbles that don't get in my way. Other times, I fight the rumble. I don't want to let go and shift the old pattern, or accept what's coming. No wonder so many of my clients think of these times of transition as something to fight through - like the rumble of a street fight; or completely avoid - like the rumble of thunder from an approaching storm.

> *"Rumble is a time to be brave. Sometimes the only way to thrive is to decide to completely embrace the rumble and allow the groove to emerge."*

Yet a new, more compelling story is emerging about this time in between. A new paradigm and new perspective. Rumble is a time to be brave; to stay open and learn; a time to suspend past judgments and remember we aren't alone. Sometimes, the only way to thrive is to decide to completely embrace the rumble; to take a deep breath and allow the groove to emerge; to find the courage to believe in the possibility between what once was and what's coming.

Back in the circle with the software engineers, ==the groove begins tugging at me, threatening to falter again.== No surprise. ==It's inevitable. Patterns shift.== Rhythms change. This time, I'll use a different technique to move the group from one groove to the next. But it's the ==focused, joyful spirit== these engineers displayed in the rumble that really calls to me. Willing participants, brave enough to share their spirit with each other. And it's that same indomitable spirit that I'm sharing in these chapters, in these stories, along with strategies and skills that will help you thrive. ==The existence of the rumble,== that space between old patterns and new pathways, ==is not in question.== The strategies to thrive in it are almost obvious. The only real question is: ==Are you willing?==

Rumble =

- *Anxiety.*
- *Self-doubt.*
- *Ambiguity.*
- *Discomfort.*
- *Vulnerability.*
- *Chaos.*

Bridge — Courage

Discover... what is emerging
- *New insights*
- *New possibilities*
- *New pathways*

Your Rumble Zone

The word 'rumble' feels like change. There's movement to the word, and a feeling of something unsettled. And it's an apt metaphor for the moments in life when change disrupts us so intensely it dominates our thoughts and weighs down our hearts. This is part of being human. We face disruption and change in our personal lives, our professional lives, our community, our family, and our world. We can manage a great deal of change and disruption – much of it does not even rise to the level of our awareness. We have a natural ability to adapt to change unconsciously. But sometimes, relationships and events require our conscious, intentional attention. This is our Rumble Zone. We know what needs attention, but are we willing to take the next step? Without attending to these disrupting rumbles, they become hindrances and hurdles to our success and happiness. When we feel stress, anxiety or sadness, it's a good time to check our Rumble Zone and notice what feels shaky, questionable or stressful. Whatever it is, it needs attention.

Reflections

Rumbles tend to show up in 2 ways: something that we seek out for ourselves (new job, new relationship, new skill) and something that life imposes on us, not by our choice (loss of job, change in relationship by another person, disease). Consider these questions to help you identify the rumbles in your life.

- What is a long-term goal you have for yourself, personally or professionally, that you have struggled to attain? (List as many as possible)

- What relationships are the most challenging for you right now? (List as many as possible)

- What is a current disruption in your life that you are dealing with because it was imposed on you? (List as many as possible)

- What are the physical cues, common thoughts or feelings you typically feel when you are trying something new or adapting to a change in direction?

As we move through the chapters of this book, use these situations as food for thought.

Chapter 2

Rally Courage

> We all have the extraordinary coded within us,
> waiting to be released.
>
> –Jean Houston

Military women and men heading into battle. African Americans marching in Selma. A child facing another round of chemotherapy. These are the images often associated with courage. Brave souls willing to face physical harm to fight for freedom, equal rights, and their life.

There is another form of courage also relevant to our everyday life, but we might be hesitant to describe these ordinary actions as courageous. A software engineer raising concerns to her manager about a flaw in strategy. An elderly neighbor seeking help for a household chore. A young man asking a date to the school prom. While there's no apparent physical risk in these acts, there are potential social risks - rejection, humiliation, or loss of perceived status. This is the type of courage I often hear about from the leaders and professionals I work with. Over the past 15 years, more and more of my clients refer to this kind of courage as one of the most important qualities needed as they face the continual shifts and demands of their fast-paced lives. Every now and then, I'm fortunate enough to witness one of those quiet acts of courage in a workshop. That's what happened on a rainy Tuesday afternoon when I met Kay.

14 Jim Boneau

The Courage to Ask

I was facilitating a seminar for 18 leaders from a high-tech company. One by one, the men and women came into the room, signed the roster, and began looking for a place to sit. I could see that many were already uncomfortable. This class had no tables to sit behind; just chairs in a semicircle. We were doing something different here. Whatever preconceived stories and judgments these leaders brought with them were already being challenged, before the class even began.

At five minutes before the published start time of the workshop, Kay enters, the last participant to come into the room. She enters in an electric wheelchair, guiding her movements with a joystick. In past workshops, I've had participants with special needs but, given my limited experience with those in wheelchairs, I make a special effort to check in with Kay. We have a good introductory conversation. She's happy to be here, both to learn and give what she can to the group. As we talk more, it's apparent she has a lot to offer - years of experience, a willingness to connect, and something else I can't quite put my finger on. But soon enough it becomes clear: Kay has brought into the room an unspoken determination to get something she deeply needs. Her courage will be a model for all of us.

The class includes structured communication exercises for the leaders to practice. These exercises are based on the T-Group work pioneered at the National Training Laboratory. I teach a few modules on self-awareness, emotional intelligence, and interpersonal communication. Everyone practices by sharing their immediate thoughts, feelings, and wants. But by the middle of the day, the group splits between those who see value in these exercises and those who think it's all a waste of time. As the leaders learn these new communication skills and are put in situations to use them, they encounter the inevitable fear and self-doubt associated with change. The change, in this case, is in applying this new approach to communication. This is their rumble moment. Are they willing to find the courage to face potential social harm by learning and practicing a new skill in a public forum?

I have mentally put Kay in the group of non-believers - someone who is thinking this is all becoming a waste of time. During the afternoon break, she asks to speak to me privately. I assume she wants to know why we are doing what we are doing. But, soon enough, I realize Kay is working at another level all together. She's assessing the situation and gathering the courage to ask for what she really wants from the group. She tells me she wants feedback from her colleagues. She wants to ask them if they believe she is less intelligent than others because she is in a wheelchair. The honesty and bravery of her question stuns me. She wants to know how she is perceived. And she is willing to muster the courage to ask the question and hear the response.

> *"Key findings recently discovered that the sections in the brain which activate in response to physical pain are the same sections of the brain that activate in response to social pain."*

As we begin the next series of activities, Kay speaks up. "I want to know how each of you perceive me as a leader when you see me in a wheelchair. Do you think I'm less intelligent and less capable of leading? Do you think I offer less value because of my visible disability?" You could hear a pin drop in the room as Kay's shocked colleagues took in the immensity of her question. The first response acknowledges her bravery to even ask the question. The second response is a quick dismissal that anyone in the room would think less of her because she's in a wheelchair. Kay looks directly at the person who made that comment. "I'm not asking anyone," she says. "I'm asking you." Before that person can reply, another participant speaks up. "When you entered the room, I recognized you. A few years ago, I worked in a related organization to yours and witnessed the outstanding quality of your leadership. I didn't think less of you when you came in here. I just wondered what happened to you and I didn't think it was appropriate to ask."

Kay opens up to the group and shares the story of how her life changed because of an accident. It's the unintended consequences of her asking the question that is becoming the true teacher as the conversations continue. One by one, participants begin to share their own stories of challenge, their personal rumble moments: recently divorced; a sibling who committed suicide; addiction; fear of loss of career. Kay's courage and the resulting conversations more than answered her question. But it's clear to me she's no longer concerned about those answers. She found the courage to ask for what she needed. And with that, she realized her leadership capability to influence others.

While the traditional definition of courage may conjure up images of daredevils leaping off buildings or soldiers heading into war, Kay demonstrated that courage also exists in everyday social situations. The courage to ask a question in class. The courage to take a stand against a strategy one believes will cause the business to be less effective. The courage to have a meaningful conversation with a spouse. All of these situations require a different type of bravery; the daring to change old patterns, learn new skills, feel emotions that are difficult. All of these are full of authentic risk. Can I really do this? What happens if I fail? What will others think of me? Navigating life's challenges often demands that we adapt; face our own limiting beliefs about our ability to cope; confront our own self-created stories of an outcome we can't possibly predict. Being willing to rumble is about meeting these fears and doubts, and ultimately rallying courage.

This connection between courage to take action that may cause physical pain (bungee jumping, for example) and the courage it takes to ask a question in a class when it may cause social embarrassment may not seem related on the surface, but they are deeply related within the grey matter of our brain. There is a great deal of scientific data on the biology of the brain and how it reacts and adapts to various stimuli. Through enhanced computer imaging of the brain, key findings recently discovered the sections in the brain responding to physical pain are the same sections in the brain responding to social pain. When we're standing on the edge of a bridge waiting to bungee jump, our sympathetic nervous system warns us of the potential for pain or death. Our instinct, buried deep within our brain and influenced by years of our own experience and millennia of evolution, tells us to avoid physical pain and stay alive. In order to actually do the bungee jump, we overcome instinct with knowledge, practice, will, and ultimately courage to take the leap. In the same manner, we consider asking a risky question which we perceive makes us vulnerable to social pain because of the answers from others. Our instincts tell us to avoid the question and stay safe. Or ask the question and run, to avoid hearing the answer. We overcome instinct with knowledge, practice, will, and ultimately courage to ask for what we want or need, as Kay did when she asked her question. In both cases, the brain, at an unconscious level, is preparing us to potentially be in pain. In physical pain, our nerve endings are the receptors of the pain and tell our brain when we experience physical pain. In social pain, our emotions are the pain receptors.

Given this research, it's no wonder one of the most common words leaders use when discussing the challenges of having a difficult conversation is 'courage'. Do I have the courage to stand up for my values when I see others acting in a way that violates my deeply held beliefs? Do I have the courage to ask for what I want or need, like Kay had? Can I endure the potential social pain of being me?

Merriam-Webster defines courage as "the mental or moral strength to venture, persevere, and withstand danger, fear, or difficulty." The mental strength comes from knowledge and experience. There are some dangers that we learn have no benefit, even if we rally courage. We learn early on, for instance, maybe from experience, we shouldn't touch the hot burner on the stove because it will result in physical harm. We get no advantage or enjoyment from that physical harm. But some dangers do reward us for the choice to be courageous. We learn we can survive those dangers (back to bungee jumping) if we have the proper circumstances. Mentally, we can develop the knowledge and skills needed to survive a challenge, like bungee jumping, that provides a payoff. But how do we rally courage when the balance between risk and payoff seems less clear? This is when moral strength is required. What values do you believe in? What do you want? What do you think is best for you, your family, your community, or your organization? And what are you willing to risk to bring those beliefs into action?

When one is willing to rumble, to step into the unknown, one is working to overcome the perception of danger and fear that goes along with any change. Most of us are comfortable where we are - even if where we are is not where we really want to be. We are surrounded by an ever evolving and changing planet: Seasons change, weather changes, landscapes change. We are surrounded by ever changing people: Hair color changes, children grow up, new people show up and others leave. However, even with all this constant change around us, as busy, task-focused people, we often believe we don't want or need to change. Rather than adapting and evolving with the world and people around us, we become stuck or in denial of the change right in front of us. This is true if the change is thrust upon us or, more surprisingly, if we signed up for this change in the first place.

The Courage to Take the First Step

That's the case for me one afternoon, as I sit under a palm tree at a park next to the airport in Honolulu, Hawaii. I have signed up to attend my very first Drum Circle Facilitation workshop. I made the choice to come. I volunteered to be here. And yet, I cannot rally the courage to walk 200 feet to introduce myself to the organizers. I don't understand my resistance. I am an experienced leader and workshop facilitator. I am a confident and successful professional. But under this palm tree, I am terrified to take the first step.

I learned about this drum circle facilitation workshop just three weeks ago. I had been facilitating corporate training for years, but I had never known about using rhythm and music for team building. My employer was hosting a worldwide conference of all the training and development staff. On the agenda of the conference was a team-building session where the group learns to play percussion instruments and make music together. It was a participatory drum circle; a family-friendly, purpose-driven event to build a sense of team among our workgroup.

The drum circle had a facilitator who would lead us through the event. The facilitator and I had an engaging conversation as I helped him set up the room. I was curious about how he got into drum circle facilitation. While not a drummer, music had always been a major part of my life – both listening and playing music. The facilitator was going to use rhythm as a team-building metaphor. One of my long-term professional goals was to become a facilitator of team building. Working in software had been rewarding, but my real dream was individual and organizational leadership development. I was intrigued by every aspect of this rhythm experience, even though the event had not yet started.

The facilitator told me he learned drum circle leadership from a man named Arthur Hull. Then, because of my obvious interest, he handed me a flyer announcing that Arthur Hull would be leading a drum circle facilitation workshop in Hawaii in three weeks. My instinct immediately cautioned me to pull back. There was too much risk here. I had walled off these dreams for years. After all, I had a good job and a great group of friends in Texas, where I lived. Yet, I knew something important was missing in my life. Love relationships had never been successful for me. I wanted a family, someone to share my life with. That part of my life didn't work at all, and I wasn't ready to discover why. It felt too risky to take a step toward these dreams. But, to be polite, I thanked the facilitator and told him I'd think about it.

The drum circle experience at the conference really impacted me. The power of this activity as a metaphor for corporate life seemed immense. But after the event, self-doubt set in as I considered actually going to Hawaii to attend the drumming workshop. The reasons for saying 'No' dominated my inner dialog. I wasn't a drummer. I didn't have time. I wouldn't get anything useful. It just didn't make any sense. All excuses for my fears. Although my life was full of rewarding experiences, something deeper continually pulled at me. Yet, I somehow felt authentic fulfillment in life was simply not for me. Accessing the courage to take steps in that direction seemed impossible.

> *"When one is willing to rumble, to step into the unknown, one is working to overcome the perception of danger and fear that goes along with any change."*

Fortunately, sometimes the courage to move forward shows up in unexpected places. A week after the corporate drum circle, I had a conversation with a friend who had just returned from a 2-year stint in the Peace Corps. She shared the challenges of her journey and the satisfaction she felt after taking that leap of faith. The courage needed to attend a week-long workshop in Hawaii seemed pale in comparison. I confirmed my registration the next day.

I flew to Hawaii with Kathy, a close friend, who joined me for a week of vacation in Maui before the workshop began. Back in Honolulu, she drove me to the park where all the drumming participants were meeting. We could hear the pounding rhythm before I even got out of the car. At the far end of the park, under a covered pavilion, twenty-five men and women were playing drums while they waited for the bus to camp. But I suddenly couldn't get out of the car. Fear took over. What in the world was I doing here? I wouldn't fit in. They were all musicians and hippies. They wouldn't like me. I was just a corporate guy. I wouldn't like them.

I turn to Kathy and admit I can't do it. I want to abandon my plans. Go sightseeing in Waikiki with her today instead. But she can see past my fear. Oddly enough, she makes an offhand remark that would turn out to be an accurate reading of the future. "Just go," she insists. "Who knows? One day, you'll probably be teaching this."

This is a pivotal moment for me. I don't believe I can rally the courage to take those 200 steps; to sign my name to the list and introduce myself to the group. Fear is clearly in control. Fear of the possibility of what good might come from attending. Fear to face myself in a completely foreign environment. I close my eyes, listening more deeply to the distant drumming. There is only one thing for me to do. Make a choice. Choose to take the first step. Just the first step. And then choose the next step and after that, the next. I thank Kathy and get out of the car, making the choice to walk toward the unknown.

Overcoming our instinct to run from pain (both social and physical) requires mental and moral strength. In this chapter, we are focusing specifically on the courage to overcome social pain when we set out on the road of change (learning something new, adapting to surroundings, or seeking to deepen a relationship). Kay had the courage to ask a question. I rallied the courage to step into the drum circle community.

In professional and personal transformational work, there are two key areas of courage that need to be explored in order to stand up to the potential social pain of living and working with others through change. First, you must know what you stand for. What is the belief, value, or priority you are compelled to address? We must have the courage to live our beliefs. Second, you can gain additional insight into your fear of living out your belief by asking this: Are you more afraid to (or does it take more courage to) speak your belief aloud to others? Or, are you more afraid to (or does it take more courage to) hear their response to your belief? We'll look at that first question, what do you stand for, in a later chapter. For now, let's explore the difference between the courage to speak your belief and the courage to hear the response.

Every day, we strive to make choices and behave in a manner that reflects our values and core beliefs. But, rarely do we speak about our values or our core beliefs. I've met thousands of leaders making choices that represent the best of humanity: offering to care for others in times of need, making the extra effort for the team, and even taking the time to sort out the recycling bin. Many times, it's easy to choose to do the right thing. However, when I provide an opportunity for leaders to reflect on their values and beliefs and then share them, they often express a sense of dread and fear about expressing them. These men and women want to walk their talk in the workplace and at home. But to declare their personal beliefs or values aloud seems too risky. These leaders admit that they are afraid of speaking their real truth. I often hear excuses like, "My actions are more important than my words" or "They should know what's important to me already" or "No one is interested in my beliefs." Maybe some of these reasons are true, but that does not diminish the importance of communicating our beliefs and letting others know what is truly important to us.

I can easily resonate with this fear because it wasn't long ago that I had to find the courage to express the truth about who I was and what I wanted. In my life, there has been no moment that required more courage than the first time I told someone I was gay.

The Courage to Tell the Truth

As John and I walk along the isolated beach in Hawaii, under the star-studded night sky, I can't ignore the heaviness in my body; the weight of a truth that can no longer go unspoken.

The timing is less than ideal. But really, when is it ever a good time to come out of the closet and admit a deep attraction to a close friend? Especially when you've been dating a woman who happens to be his close friend. This was supposed to be an amazing week of drumming on the beach in Hawaii. But it was destined to create a massive upheaval and rumble in my life and in the lives of my closest friends.

I had met John a year ago, during the first drum facilitation workshop I attended in Hawaii. We were like brothers reuniting after lifetimes apart. John possessed a strength of purpose I had never seen in another human being. He was eager to learn as much as possible about drumming facilitation and building a business. I shared those same interests. Our brief connection in Hawaii led to a trip to Seattle, where John lived, for more drumming. A few months later, I quit my job in Texas and moved to Seattle. John and I began working together in drumming circles. And he introduced me to his friends and community. That's when I met his friend, Stacia, who I started dating. The three of us were inseparable that summer. Then, one day when the three of us were in the park playing drums, John took off his shirt. I looked at them both and admitted to myself, then and there, I was gay.

Now, a year after first meeting John, sitting next to him under the stars, I'm about to do something that could potentially destroy everything. He has no idea what I'm about to say. And I don't have any idea how to say it. We start talking about the opening session of this 10-day drumming facilitation workshop we're both attending. Today, over a hundred people from all over the world shared personal stories about their lives and their commitment to building community through rhythm. I was deeply moved by the honesty of the group. So who am I to think I can authentically participate in this workshop and serve this drumming community without being completely honest myself? I don't have the strength to carry my secret until we are back in Seattle. To make it through these next 10 days, I must tell John. I don't expect any kind of reciprocation from him. This isn't about him at all. This is about me speaking the truth.

> "*Most of us are comfortable with where we are - even if where we are is not where we really want to be.*"

I stop the chit chat and take a deep breath. My heart is pounding. I feel as though I am standing on the edge of a cliff. The words come tumbling out of my mouth. I admit my attraction to him. I tell him how strong and real these feelings are. He stares back at me in total silence. "I had to tell you tonight," I say, "because if I don't own who I am now,

I never will. And if I don't own this truth, the weight of my hypocrisy in this community will destroy me." It is the most vulnerable statement I've ever made. And not just to anyone but to a man I believe I'm in love with. This is the most truthful moment of my life: asking to be seen for who I am for the very first time.

John keeps staring at me. Finally, he speaks but it's only questions. When did this happen? Has it happened before? What about Stacia? Who have you told?

I tell him about the day in the park. John lets me know definitively that he's never felt this way toward me, or toward any other man. "This is your situation," he insists, "not mine." Yes, it's mine. My courageous act. John's response is less important to me because now, on the right side of truth, I'm more deeply connected to who I am. I'm no longer able to continue the charade. I'm overwhelmed with the need to be known, to relieve myself of this burden I've been carrying for longer than I ever realized. There was no other option than to find the courage to tell John. I never even considered what his response would be. I didn't care if he hugged me or stormed away. I just knew the pain of not being seen for who I am was greater than the anticipated pain from him and the rest of my community. Whatever the consequences, I was willing to speak the truth and risk the social pain. And in this situation, the risk was well worth the reward. I was able to be honest with myself, John and Stacia. That truth built a foundation for long-lasting, truthful friendships that I share with both of them still today.

Why are we so hesitant to be honest about the way we live each day? Why does it take courage to speak out? I see two emerging causes for this fear: publicly being on record (the reality of our hyper-connected social media world) and the emotional impact of being truly seen by those we live and work with in our community. I am a gay man. I live in a long-term partnership with a man. We are active members of our community in Seattle. I travel to cities all over the US and the world. I lead workshops discussing authenticity, integrity, and trust. And yet, when someone asks about my family and home life, I always need courage to answer their question honestly. It feels as if I have to come out again and again. I feel fear because I'm sharing who I am, what I stand for, and what I believe. I'm opening myself to be truly seen by another and that ramps up all kinds of emotions. Each time, I must find the courage to speak my truth in front of others. And, while my years of life experience now make me less concerned about their responses, having the spotlight completely on me as I state my truth can still be, at times, terrifying.

The Courage to Hear the Response

Sometimes we need courage to truly listen to the response of others. That courage is often needed most when we care for and respect the other person. We may be afraid the other person might say something that hurts our feelings. So we put off conversations because we don't want to hear their response and feel the emotions that would trigger. I know this fear too well. In the second year of graduate school, something happened that taught me the pain of not being brave enough to listen would be greater than the pain I feared in hearing someone's honest response.

We had a visiting leadership coach and professional facilitator speak to the graduate department about the business of organizational development. This guy was running the kind of company I dreamed to be a part of. He was doing the work I wanted to do. He was someone I wanted to connect with. At one point in the session, we broke into small groups, had a discussion, and were invited by the facilitator to share with the entire room the insights from our small group discussion. I stood up for my group and gave a brief summary of what we talked about. Afterwards, I stood in line to introduce myself and thank him for the inspiring session. I had no intention of asking for advice or mentoring. But he told me he wanted to offer some feedback. "When you gave your group summary," he said, "I could see that you were clearly a gifted master facilitator." His comment took me by surprise. I didn't know what to say, so I thanked him and hurried out of the room.

I stood in the hallway for a few minutes reflecting on his words. He saw something professionally in me that I desperately wanted someone to see. I wanted to go back in and share my dream of doing what he was doing, ask for his advice, but I was too afraid to hear his response. I literally ran away, because I didn't have the courage to hear what he would say. I assumed that sharing my dreams and expectations would be too much. Those were the thoughts going through my head as I stood by myself in the hallway, watching this opportunity fade. And then, in an instant, I made a different choice. I decided to rally the courage to hear his response. I walked into the room. He greeted me with, "You're back?" And this time I didn't hesitate. I boldly asked him to consider hiring me for a role where I could work for his clients. The moment I finished speaking, my fear hit a crescendo. I was afraid of hearing his response, because I assumed this one conversation was the only way I could ever be successful. I assumed this was the only moment I'd ever have in my life and there would be no other opportunities. Were my dreams about to get torched because of his response? Or would this ignite an amazing opportunity?

But, once again, I make a different choice. I find the courage to face the narrative I'm creating in my own head. I find the courage to hear what he has to say. And one month later, I'm working for his company, giving a keynote speech at an annual leadership conference. My courage to ask for what I wanted and the courage to hear the response were key elements of changing a life-long pattern of resistance and self-doubt.

Taking a step towards a new path in life or pursuing a desire to deepen a relationship always comes with risk. Am I capable of doing this? Will I be happy in this new role, in this new career, in being known even more by those in my life? We can do all the research, all the planning, and all the preparation. But then, in the moment when the choice is present, when we feel the fear, we must find courage. Courage to ask, courage to speak up, courage to listen. And then we must find it again and again and again.

Courage
- *To Ask*
- *To Take Action*
- *To Tell Truth*
- *To Hear Response*

Your Rumble Zone

As we proceed through these chapters, we will examine your rumbles through a variety of strategies. Just as in a drum circle, variety and diversity gives us better results. Drum circles tend to have fuller, richer and more interesting grooves with a large variety of percussion instruments available to play. Lower sounding drums are like a heartbeat. Drums that make a higher pitched sound are the melody line of the groove. Bells, shakers, and wood blocks are the spices that jazz up the spaces between the notes of the drum. Each of those sounds comes together dynamically to create a groove in the moment.

Navigating change is similar, in that many elements come together dynamically to create a path to something new. In the drum circle, the facilitator might ask for the bells and shakers to play more loudly, or for the low drums to play by themselves. The facilitator is attempting to balance all the sounds to make the best music possible. We are going to take a similar approach in the application of the rumble strategies. Some situations require more courage, others more empathy. You are the facilitator balancing the strategies needed to thrive in the rumble.

Reflections

To apply each of these strategies, you must first focus your reflections on a particular situation in your rumble zone. Use these questions to identify a situation and how you can rally courage.

- If you were afraid of a rumble in your current rumble zone, which one would it be?

- Is the fear more related to you (your ability, being known, speaking your truth) or is the fear more related to others (their judgments, reactions, potential impact on them)?

Once you identify which holds more potential fear for you, spend some time writing about the potential fears. Be as specific as possible about the fear, including long-term implications that could be contributing to the fear. End your time writing by answering 'Yes' or 'No' to this statement: I choose to bring my best effort to this rumble.

If you are willing to rumble, you are willing to assemble the resources necessary to take the courageous step.

- What skills do you need to learn to support your courageous act?

- What relationships will support you before, during and after you choose courage?

- How can you care for yourself to ensure you bring your best to the rumble?

- What does ==courage== look like in your rumble? What are you saying? What are you doing? What is the best response possible? What is the worst?

- What is the most ==potent next step== you can take to move yourself towards the courageous act?

- How do you ==care for yourself== physically, emotionally, and spiritually when you deplete your resources in this courageous act?

Chapter 3

Be Present

> When you are patient enough to stop,
> look and listen, asking what to do, you will
> always be shown how to do it.
>
> –Iyanla Vanzant

It's day two of a three-day leadership and Emotional Intelligence workshop I'm teaching for an American manufacturing giant, when the entire room's mobile phones erupt in a cacophony of beeps and ringing. The setting is the Super Bowl of training events for senior leaders, and the biggest corporate training deployment I've ever been a part of. I'm one of 6 facilitators, each working with a small subset of the 200 executives attending this workshop. There are twenty leaders in my room. The event alternates between classrooms, where participants divide into smaller groups for more intimate discussions, and the main lecture hall, where all two hundred gather in a single, state-of-the-art training center. This is a highly structured event, with a very specific curriculum. But the simultaneous beeping and ringing of all the smartphones signals something very serious. I can see it in the confusion and panic on the faces of these men and women. An unexpected change is occurring that has the potential to alter the careers of most of the attendees of this workshop. I pause for a moment, considering how to respond. I can continue teaching the required curriculum or address what's happening right now. For me, the choice is clear.

To thrive in the ambiguity of expected or unexpected change - whether it's an interrupted training event, a conflict with a colleague, or a long-term plan to turn around a business – demands that we clearly understand what's happening around us and inside ourselves in the moment. Before we can adapt or take any kind of action, we must know what we are reacting to. While there will always be information about what to do or say next, the real challenge is to be present enough to become conscious of that vital information. If we're aware enough, we can learn from what's happening around us, adapt to it, and use everything as a stepping stone to a more desirable pathway.

The Benefits of Mindfulness

The concept of being present and mindful has moved far beyond the yoga studio and meditation center to professionals in business and beyond. Media outlets like the New York Times, NPR, and local newspapers have published countless articles on the benefits of practicing mindfulness; everything from increased creativity and stress reduction to improved relationships and health. Yet, when we read these articles, it's like reading about the benefits of exercise or eating right. We know what it takes to have a healthy physical body, but do we make that better choice in the moment? The same holds true for being present. We read that practicing mindfulness is good for us, but when the circumstances arise, are we actually doing it? The act of stopping for an instant to ask ourselves if we are present is, in and of itself, an act of mindfulness. And that's the point about being present - it's always a choice. Exercising that choice in a difficult situation allows us to see and interpret the additional information available to us: the look of discouragement on the face of a friend who can use a kind, supportive word; the anxious expression of a colleague who needs encouragement to say something he's afraid to say.

> *"To make the most effective choices and take the most effective actions, we must be aware of what is going on right now: We must be present to what is."*

This is the real benefit of being present. When we see, hear and feel what is truly happening outside, as well as inside ourselves, we have access to essential information that can ultimately inform how we move forward. Having access to more information and more choices is an advantage in change.

That's exactly what happened when I heard the explosion of beeps and ringing in the workshop. I made a choice to stop and pay much closer attention to what was unfolding. In the middle of a rumble - that time between changing patterns and an emerging new path - even the obvious, like smartphones ringing, can be hard to notice, especially if we're lost in our own anxious thoughts and feelings. In addition to what's obvious, there are also the less clear and more subtle messages being sent – confused looks, whispering, lack of eye contact, restless body language. If we can be present in the moment to what's going on in ourselves and around us, we can gather a wealth of critical data offering insights on how to move forward.

The beeping and ringing continue. I make the decision to stop the planned curriculum and ask the group what's going on. The information is disconcerting to say the least. It seems the industrial giant they all work for has just announced it's selling its core business line in an effort to restructure. Over a third of the attendees here work in that line of business. Their jobs, which a moment before were secure, are now in serious jeopardy. The last thing these men and women want to do now is listen to a lecture on leadership or participate in a mundane role-playing activity. The current moment is the most challenging I could have ever imagined for a class scenario. Only this isn't a role play. It's real life.

The voices inside my own head are also demanding my attention. What am I going to do? How am I going to get through all the remaining curriculum? The other facilitators must be managing their groups better than me.

The first step to practicing mindfulness in this situation is the simple, yet powerful act of becoming aware of my conflicting thoughts and feelings. I want to be of service to this group. I want to run out of here and ask someone else what to do. I want to rise to the occasion and use the skills I'm trained to apply. If all this is going on right now in my own head, I can only imagine the thoughts and emotions of those affected by this startling news.

As is often the case in times of great stress, I feel pressure to solve the problem happening for those in the room. Of course, I quickly realize

I can't. Attempting to solve their problem would be the biggest mistake I could make. This crisis of career aspirations shifting, families relocating, and futures on hold are not problems I can solve in this moment. I bring myself back to the present moment and think about what I need to do right now to be of service to these men and women. None of us are going to solve these long-term problems. The best thing I could do for the group is to slow them down, name the moment, and offer them an opportunity to express their own thoughts, feelings, and needs.

But to do that, I need to get them all connected to what is actually happening right now, instead of fantasizing and future-tripping about the unknown impact of this announcement.

I ask everyone to turn to the person sitting beside them and discuss four questions: How are you personally impacted by the news? What are the immediate implications for you specifically? What are your current thoughts and feelings? How is the company living or not living its values in the announcement?

It's important that each participant connect to what's happening inside themselves before they can even begin to address what's happening around them.

Out of the Story and Into the Moment

As human beings, we are story-making machines. It's how we continue to survive and adapt to our ever-changing world. We take a single event and instinctually assign judgment, blame, cause and effect; we create scenarios that are often much worse than the impending reality. We then begin to act out that new story. But ultimately, we are acting out something that is completely made up, and not what's unfolding right in front of us. We're making choices based on a future state that has not yet occurred, rather than on the current information. To make the most effective choices and take the most effective actions, we must see what is going on right now: *We must be present to what is.*

Of course, it's often impossible to live every single moment of our lives with this level of mindfulness. To be completely present in all situations can be exhausting. In my work as a leadership coach, I limit the number of clients I schedule per day, because I know how difficult it is to be present in every conversation for such a long period of time.

The practice of coming back to the moment is a muscle to be exercised and developed. Meditation is not about being quiet and empty headed; it's about silently acknowledging when a random thought enters our head, and then coming back to the present moment. Then doing that same thing again and again. By building this muscle, it gets easier to catch those random thoughts which take us away from what's actually happening.

Given our tendency to future-trip about a made-up story, I invite the class participants to reflect and share their thoughts and feelings. After a few minutes of quiet, authentic conversations begin to emerge. Stories of anger, confusion, and frustration. Concern for colleagues and friends. As the candid sharing continues, my boss - the lead facilitator - comes into the room asking for my attention. I'm glad to see him and eager to hear his plan on how we navigate this sudden crisis. He informs me that the client wants to bring all the smaller groups back into the main conference area to read the formal announcement from the company. I'm happy to hear that, because it will give everyone a chance to gain some much needed clarity. My boss goes on to tell me that, after the announcement, the client also wants us to do something to get the entire group back on track with the required curriculum. Truthfully, I'm relieved. "So what's your plan?" I ask. He pauses for a moment, then smiles. "I'm giving the room to you," he says. "It's your job to get everyone refocused on the workshop." I'm thrown for a moment. This is not the answer I expected. "But what do you want me to do?" I ask. As he walks out of the room, he replies, "You'll figure it out."

Suddenly I'm hyper aware that everyone in my small room is watching me to see my reaction to a conversation most of them heard. My thoughts are swirling around in my brain. I don't know what I'm going to say to the whole group. I don't have enough time to plan. I'm not sure I can do this. I need reassurance from my colleagues.

What I do know, however, is I'll be most effective as a facilitator if I can slow down, right now, and acknowledge what's going on for me. By doing so, I also feel a deeper sense of excitement and confidence. It's clear to me the best way to serve these executives whose world has just been turned upside down is to recognize the difficult situation they're in, and invite them to come back to the here and now. As we file out of the classroom to the auditorium, I'm certain that if I can truly be in the moment, I'll know what to say when I step on that stage.

> "*We aren't fixing the situation, but we see it. We name it. We feel it. As a group and as individuals, we are mindful of the moment we are in, not distracted by a made-up future.*"

Being mindful does not require a college education or special degrees. The only requirement is the willingness to practice self-awareness and look more deeply at what's going on inside and around you. Being present is ultimately the act of stepping out of your stories about the future and the past and, instead, seeing and feeling what is happening now.

As I stand on the stage being fitted with a microphone, the auditorium is quickly filling up with all 200 participants. Imagine a corporate conference room that is a combination of an IMAX movie theater, a high-tech classroom, and a NASA control room that seats 500. Once again, I notice my internal judgements and doubts. Will this mindfulness approach really work here? This isn't a yoga class or a drum circle or a San Francisco start-up. I'm standing in front of the pinnacle of corporate leaders, who work for a titan of American industry.

But, over and over, I bring myself back to the present. I look out at the rows of tables, reaching up like the high school football stadiums where I used to play my trombone during halftimes. Making that connection gives me comfort. All the tables are outfitted with individual reading lights and microphones, so each executive can speak to the group. Yes, it's a big room, but a classroom like any other. That also gives me comfort. As my mind drifts, I keep bringing myself back to what's happening right in front of me. And that allows me the clarity and freedom to not act out of fear, but instead to trust my instinct to invite the participants to do the same.

After the client reads the official news from the company, it's my cue to take center stage. I speak from my heart, naming the truth we know in this moment and challenging anything beyond that. I remind them there is more unknown than known about the future, and there is more unknown than known about the now. I invite all of us to gain awareness of what we can know right now - not what we're speculating about the future. I give everyone time to reflect, to share with one another; to share with the whole group. It becomes clear there is nowhere to go and nothing to do but listen to what is going on for each and every one of them.

And, once again, I witness that being present, practicing mindfulness, is a powerful act. The room softens, the tension releases. We're saying the truth out loud and no one is running away. We aren't fixing the situation, but we see it. We name it. We feel it. As a group and as individuals, we are mindful of the moment we are in, not distracted by a made-up future.

The large group session ends and we all return to our individual classrooms. One of the participants raises his hand to speak. An MBA from an Ivy League school, he's been a Doubting Thomas all day, quick to share his strong opinions on leadership principles and why Emotional Intelligence is a waste of time. But his comments surprise everyone, including me. "I get it now," he admits. "At other times when we had to deal with bad news in this company, we dealt with it by completely ignoring it. And then it went underground and everyone eventually felt worse. But today, we did something different. We acknowledged the difficulty; we spoke the truth about what was happening. And, while we didn't fix or change or solve anything, I feel better. I'm ready to take the next step."

When you're willing to rumble, then you are courageous enough to look at the current moment clearly, as well as acknowledge your own thoughts and feelings. You're also willing to recognize what's going on in the minds and hearts of the people around you. Transformation does not occur unless we are present to what is happening inside and out.

As a strategy for thriving in the time of rumble, being present is an invitation to meet and feel the fear and insecurities, as uncomfortable as they might be. Those are only the surface emotions playing out when we are breaking old patterns. Underneath these feelings are gateways to valuable information: clues to what ties us to the old way of being; shame about our past failures; vulnerability about trying something new but not getting it right the first time. When we can become aware of these influences from the past, we can name them in the present. Naming something from our past that is limiting us today tends to take the bite out of it. We see the old story isn't true anymore; we see the tragic future we predict is not true either. In the current moment, there is only genuine possibility, potential, and a new pathway leading to where we want to be.

Presence:
- Attentive Now
- Listening to Rhythms
- Subtle Shifts
- Unique Rhythm

Your Rumble Zone

Mindfulness is being attentive to what's happening now, not remembering the past or planning the future, but fully engaged in what is actually happening. To be mindful is not to overthink a situation and get lost in your thoughts. As soon as you start to overthink a situation, you run the very high risk of becoming less aware of your surroundings. Playing in an improvisational drum circle offers a unique opportunity to see, hear, and feel what it's like to be present to your surroundings and the consequences of over-thinking.

In a drum circle, participants are invited to share their unique beat on their drum. There are no rhythmic patterns to remember. Instead, the drummers are listening to the rhythms of the group. They listen for space to contribute to the group's song. The drummers play a drum beat that blends into the existing rhythmic flow. Overthinking will kill the groove before it even starts. Not listening to the subtle shifts in others' patterns causes us to miss the clues of the oncoming change in the groove. Being present in the drum circle allows us to hear all the different rhythms and sounds. Mindfulness in the drum circle allows us to tap into our unique rhythm.

Reflections

Mindfulness is a muscle we can build. The unfortunate part is, it takes mindfulness to build mindfulness.

Your moment of mindfulness is about right now, not some far-off rumble. Stop now. Set a timer on your phone for 1 minute. Start the timer and get present with yourself.

- Notice your surroundings. What do you see, hear, feel, taste or smell? How does the seat and floor feel underneath you? How are you breathing? If you get distracted and your mind wanders, then you are no longer present with your surroundings.

  Mindfulness keeps your mind on the task of noticing what's around you. When you mindfully catch your thoughts wandering, just say "now" and come back to observing the moment.

When the timer stops, start it again right away, and for the next minute write down the answers to the following question:

- What are you thinking, feeling, and wanting right now?
- Do not stop writing for a full sixty seconds.

When the timer stops, start it again right away, and for the next minute, do the following:

Put your palms together and rub your hands back and forth.

- How does it feel?
- What sound do you hear?

- What thoughts or judgments are in your head, taking you away from the sound?

When the timer stops, start it again right away, and for the next minute, do the following:

- Use your hands to tap your lap like you are playing a drum. Use your full hand, then use just a finger, then tap the side of your lap – experiment with the sounds you can make.

- How does it feel?

- What sound do you hear?

- What thoughts or judgments are in your head, taking you away from the sound?

When the timer stops, start it again right away, and for this final minute, sit in silence.

- When you notice your mind racing with thoughts, quickly rub your hands or tap your lap to bring you back to the moment.

- The practice is to catch yourself when you start to spin out of the here and now.

These are examples of exercises you can do to strengthen your ability to be present and, in doing so, gain access to all the information available in every moment.

Chapter 4

Share Your Point of View

> "Be transparent. Let's build a community that allows hard questions and honest conversations so we can stir up transformation in one another."
>
> –Germany Kent

The view from inside the nuclear medicine machine is not one to brag about. The hospital does not allow a phone or tablet and there's not even a built-in screen offering a preselected movie for distraction. There are no windows in the room. There is artwork incorporated into the ceiling tiles, but the low hum of the machine does not sound like the crashing waves I want to hear looking at the view they painted on the ceiling tiles. To be scanned in the nuclear medicine machine requires me to lie still and have the machine move me 20 inches, very slowly, over an hour and a half. But this isn't my first time in the nuclear medicine machine, and I have come prepared. The first time I was in this machine, they were diagnosing the extent of my thyroid cancer. They found cancer all over my neck and lungs and, of course, in my thyroid gland. But surgery and radioactive iodine treatment had reduced that cancer to almost nothing. At least that is my hope, and this test will either confirm or dash my hope. Given the situation, I need more than the artwork on the ceiling to distract my thoughts.

My buddy, John has driven me to the appointment and agreed to sit with me throughout the time of the test. John, newspaper in hand, is ready to read it out loud, cover to cover, as the starting point for my distraction. After the news and weather, John reads an editorial article written by a local pastor, Anthony B. Robinson. The title of the article is "Being a Grown Up". We laugh at the title, but only out of joy for the great find. John and I share a personal and professional interest in living intentionally and this article is something we both want to know beyond its headline. In summary, Robinson wrote about his hunches on what it takes to be a grown up.

1. Understand it's not about you
2. Have the capacity to say something unpopular
3. Recognition that life is complex and tragic

These simple principles resonate deeply with me. Robinson's three hunches will ultimately become an inspiration for my personal and professional point of view. They give voice to a perspective I operate from but had never, up until this time, articulated as simply and profoundly.

What Is a Point of View?

What is a point of view? And why is having a point of view helpful in overcoming the rumble of change?

For our purposes, a point of view can be defined as an opinion, an attitude, or a particular way of considering something. In navigating change, your point of view is one of many, as everyone involved in the change has one. In other words, a point of view can be described as an on-going working hypothesis one person has about something as contrasted to the on-going working hypothesis another person has.

There are countless circumstances where having and expressing a point of view is central: an educated doctor sharing her assessment with a patient; a concerned family member expressing to a sibling their opinion about long-term care for their mother; a passionate colleague giving feedback about an important project to a team.

Life requires us to share our point of view with other people all the time. We often do this for the purpose of coming to some kind of agreement on how to move forward in a situation. Yet circumstances involving multiple points of view are often the place where an impending rumble might begin. When we make a choice to share a genuine opinion or perspective with others, who also have their own unique point of view, we're entering territory that will inevitably have some rough and tumble. One person may have trouble articulating their point of view and get frustrated. The other person may have difficulty understanding the first point of view and feel threatened. Yet it's necessary and valuable to be able to navigate these rough waters. We will always be interacting with different points of view. And to do any successful navigation, we must know where we're starting. We must begin by discovering or understanding our own point of view.

Investigating a Point of View

As I sit up from the nuclear scan table, those three ideas continue to bounce around in my head. And I'm more than happy to distract myself from all the fearful emotions about this cancer diagnosis fighting for my attention. I'm eager to explore how these principles of being a grown-up are relevant in my current circumstances. It seems like navigating the health care system with cancer is as good a time as any to show up as a grown up.

But the author's first principle - it's not all about me - seems farther from my truth than anything else. At this moment, it clearly is all about me – my cancer, my scan, my needs. Yet according to the article, I'm not really showing up as a grown up. An interesting point of view that I don't quite agree with at the moment.

> *"Life requires us to share our point of view with other people all the time."*

The second principle has to do with saying the things that are difficult to say. I'd had lots of practice with that one over the past year. It was difficult the first time I told a friend about the cancer. In fact, it was difficult every first time I told someone. Difficult because it made it more real; because it often brought up emotion for both of us; because it was an acknowledgment of the sadder side of life. I seemed to be having more grown up types of conversations over the past year than ever before. Coming out at 35 years old presented many opportunities for me to say something that might be perceived as unpopular. Both cancer and my sexuality have provided me lots of practice in speaking difficult truths.

The last principle the author referenced in his article is recognizing the complexity and tragedy of life. The complexity of life had shown itself to me in full form over the past few years. I went from a director role in a software company living in Dallas to an unemployed cancer patient living in Seattle. And now, because of this illness, I have a much more personal understanding of life's harshest tragedies. But the awareness I bring to the battle with cancer has been a teacher like no other, painfully illuminating aspects of my life I never really wanted to deeply examine: regret for what I hadn't yet accomplished personally and professionally; sadness and shame for waiting much too long to accept myself. Yes, I certainly have recognized the complexity and tragedy of life so far.

Reflecting on these three principles and my current situation, I can see that the evidence points to the fact that I could be perceived as a grown up. I feel a sense of comfort and accomplishment, knowing I'm able to see my life now through the lens of this point of view. But I still have trouble resolving the first principle – it's not all about me. Right now, from the doctors to the medical staff to my friends, it is all about me. However, if I want to see myself as a grown up, based on Robinson's article, I need to consider that this cancer diagnosis is somehow not all about me. If it's not about me, then it must be about someone else – in this case, those in my life who are helping me navigate the treatment of this disease. They were feeling sad and scared; they have been generous with their time. It's about me and it's about them – it's a paradox.

These principles were expanding in scope. They are more than principles to be an adult. They are principles to be an adult who wants to live connected to and in relationships with others. A fundamental point of view seems to exist in the author's thesis: To be a grown up is to live in community while nurturing our relationships with others. Yes, this has always been a core truth for me. I've expressed it in many ways over the years - professionally as a teacher and personally in building a strong foundation of community. If nurturing relationships is an axiom for being a grown up, then I can more easily accept that it's not always about me, even though in this moment it seems like it is. Nonetheless, my understanding still feels a bit incomplete. But, in the coming months, everything would make a lot more sense.

Living Up to a Point of View

Having a point of view is one thing but to live a point of view is about exercising it daily in your life. It's about using it as a lens through which you make decisions. It's about using it as a basis to help others understand how you see the world. Living a point of view is about calling on that perspective in times of deep change to be the compass that helps set direction for where you are going.

Fast forward 2 years. I've been cancer free since that day in the nuclear medicine lab. My prognosis was outstanding. Test results showed no cancer cells remaining in my body. The doctor told me to go live the rest of my life and count myself fortunate for having a type of cancer that is treatable. I was thrilled with the new lease on life, but there was another side to the defeat of cancer. I felt unsettled, restless, and disturbed. Facing cancer had forced me to look at my life and brought up uncomfortable realizations: not having the courage to pursue important dreams or authentically live as the person I was made to be. Having defeated this illness, I felt a mix of relief and responsibility, joy and sadness, hope and despair. What was I going to do now?

Robinson's principles loomed large in my mind and heart. I made the decision I was going to actively and consciously be a grown-up. And my starting place would be solidifying my point of view on how I wanted to live. My goals were clear: To live a life as a proud gay man, with a loving partner. To facilitate leadership workshops for the best organizations on the planet. To build a caring community that is connected to a common set of values.

I had some aspects of this in my life already, but this post-cancer time was a key moment to explore things more deeply, break old patterns, and generate new pathways of success.

The three principles about being an adult were relevant to me, but my understanding of them was still incomplete. To expand my point of view, I decided to pursue a graduate degree at the Leadership Institute of Seattle (LIOS) in Applied Behavioral Science. That experience led me even deeper into what it means to be a grown-up.

> "*Circumstances involving multiple points of view are often the place where an impending rumble might begin.*"

I found almost all the curriculum at LIOS to be compelling. Change management, emotional intelligence, human relationships, interpersonal skills, diversity, coaching, organizational development and facilitation were some of the subjects we learned over the two years. I discovered a great deal of overlap between my current work as a facilitator, the curriculum at LIOS, and my life philosophies. The story of how these crystallized is the story of how I came to fully understand my point of view.

In the years since first hearing the article on being a grown up, I had continued to work with those three principles. While they were relevant in many areas of my life, I found the principles particularly useful in discussing the art of facilitating a group.

I've been a group process facilitator all my life. I certainly didn't know the term "group process facilitator" or think of myself as one until more recently. At 16 years old, I led retreats for other teens attending my church. I continued that type of work through college, becoming more and more skilled at leading groups through learning experiences. I didn't know group facilitation could be a profession, so I pursued software engineering post-college. While working for a software company, I learned about opportunities to be a trainer and facilitator. Now, after years of corporate and community-based facilitation work, I was starting to develop my own point of view on what it takes to become a masterful facilitator. And it starts with being a grown up.

Facilitating a group through any type of learning process is complex. As the facilitator, I don't feel I'm acting with integrity if I'm asking those I'm teaching to do something I don't strive to live every day. Listening, leading, and connecting are also my goals as a facilitator. But I always need to remember that the learning experience is not about me; it's about the men and women sitting in the room. Robinson's principle #1 clearly applies here. As a facilitator, I'm not in front of the room to serve my own ego. I'm there to shine the spotlight on the leaders in the room. To be a masterful facilitator of learning means operating under the knowledge that it's not about me.

Principle #2 also comes directly into play during my coaching and facilitating, because it's my job to provide honest feedback to individuals and organizations about their skills and dynamics. This often requires naming out loud uncomfortable or unpopular truths. There was the time I told the executive VP of a financial services company that he was treating those around him more like an ATM machine than human beings. On another occasion, I had to address racial biases that were identified in interview sessions. When an organization truly wants to transform, when they are willing to rumble, I'm required to have a point of view and share it – regardless of its popularity.

And finally, to work towards masterful group facilitation, my mindset has to include the frame of life's complexities: The complexity of an individual working a high-pressure job, with family responsibilities, striving to be an effective leader of people. These individuals are working in an environment that is competitive, global, ever changing, and full of different personalities. These clients are successful adults, living full lives. They're dealing with immense complexity. What's more, their level of awareness of what's happening in the learning process is probably not as informed as mine – I'm the learning professional in the room. Not only is their reality complex, but my reality of facilitating 30 others in a multi-day experiential learning workshop is exponentially complex. Thus, Principle #3.

Field Testing a Point of View

The characteristics of a grown-up and the characteristics of masterful facilitation were lining up well – and yet there was something still incomplete. My professional point of view about facilitating and my personal point of view about how to live my life were still not 100% clear to me. Since I had found a paradox in principle #1, I became curious about the remaining principles.

A field test seemed in order. Since I was starting an intensive series of workshops for three global clients, I would use the backdrop of the principles of being an adult as a lens to reflect on the effectiveness of my facilitation work with the groups.

The first step of my field test occurred leading a workshop for a financial institution. We were about midway through the first day and I was introducing the concept of coaching as a tool leaders can use for the development of others. The skills I teach for coaching are, at their core, good interpersonal skills, focused on helping the other person have a profound shift in their belief in themselves. These are good skills, not only for the workplace, but for all relationships. The only reservation I have is about coaching your spouse. I told the group of how my partner at home, Eric, always senses when I shift to coach mode. "Don't use those Jedi tricks on me, Jim!" The class had a good laugh, and I made my point. Yet, it seemed to me that I had somehow violated principle #1 and made it about me.

When that lecture was over, one of the participants came over. He told me that, in all the classes he's attended over the past 20 years, he'd never seen another gay man speak so openly about their partner to make a work-related point. He shared how much he still holds back talking about his personal life, even though his colleagues all know he's gay. "You showed me that my limits are self-imposed," he said, "and that I can make a different choice."

In that moment, the paradox of Principle #1 was confirmed. To be a masterful facilitator, I had to remember it's not about me, and yet it's all about me: the story and vulnerability I offered demonstrated what's acceptable to include in a field of discussion. The extent to which I opened up became the measure of the boundaries of what is possible in the class.

Paradox tells us that the exact opposite of an idea may also be true. It's a both/and rather than either/or type of mindset. Understanding paradox helped me evolve and understand my own point of view. Paradox helps me better understand my relationship to others. Their actions and choices are not about me; they're about their own lives, their beliefs, their values, their needs, and emotions. Yet, my actions are something others respond to. The success of my work as a coach and facilitator is not about me, and yet it is about me.

The power of paradox continued to impact my point of view during another trip. A colleague and I were facilitating a workshop in India for an audience of Indian leaders and engineers of an American-based software company. Leading a workshop overseas always requires me to expand my American point of view; it's usually an invitation for me to operate more in line with the cultural and workplace norms of the country I'm visiting. This became evident on the first day of class. As an experienced facilitator, I give great importance to the value of time, specifically the start time of meetings and workshops. It's not so much about beginning right on time, but about actively respecting everyone's demanding schedules. As workshop leaders, we have a full agenda to cover in a short period of time. And the participating leaders have hectic businesses to run. Effectively using the time allotted is something we can do to help improve the learning experience.

However, in India, time is measured differently. While the published start of the workshop was 8:30 am, there were individuals trickling in until 9:15 AM. My first thought was that 8:30 am might be too early a start time for engineers. In my experience teaching in the states, tech company engineers generally arrive late in the morning and work late into the evening. Consequently, I asked the class if they would prefer a later start time. My co-facilitator and I agreed to delay the start time for day two of the workshop until 9:00 am. The understanding was that everyone would show up by 9:00 am so we could begin class together. All participants nodded their heads as well as agreeing verbally. I congratulated my co-facilitator for our teamwork in making a call that would best serve the group's learning experience. What happened on day two certainly served the learning process, but not exactly the learning we expected.

The next morning at 9:00 AM, the room sat empty. Not one of the participants was present for our newly agreed start time. My co-facilitator and I were livid. How could this have happened? Not only had we been specific about the start time and requested verbal commitments, but the curriculum for that day focused on leadership, accountability, and integrity. And yet, the exact opposite was being displayed by the group's lack of follow-through. My co-facilitator and I put two chairs at the front of the room, sat down, and waited in silence for the leaders to arrive.

At 9:02 the first person walked in, stunned to see an empty room. I told him to take a seat while we waited, in silence, for everyone else to arrive. It was 9:25 AM before the last participant showed up. Even though we were both very angry, we also knew there was a genuine learning opportunity to be seized here about trust, integrity, and accountability. Our plan was to simply report to the class, without blame or emotion, the impact this broken agreement had on us; how it potentially damaged the trust between all of us. While sharing that was certainly uncomfortable for me, it was also necessary. Leaders need to see the impact of not staying true to their commitments.

Yet, we didn't dominate the discussion with our point of view. We wanted to provide an opportunity for the group to assess the situation on their own. Would accountability, self-management, and group leadership emerge from the class without being directed or coached by us? Of course, I desperately wanted to tell them what they needed to do to be better leaders. But, in the end, that was their work to do. I knew my role was to keep quiet and let silence guide them. I knew it would be much more powerful and effective if it came from within the group itself. After some initial defensiveness and attempts to draw out our anger, a leader stood up and began a conversation about the group's accountability. He insisted that the group own up to what really happened. "We can't blame this on our facilitator's lack of understanding about our culture," he said. "They're guests in our country and here to help us. We agreed to show up at a certain time and then we failed on that commitment."

Slowly the conversation shifted from blame and defensiveness to self-reflection and responsibility. It was a powerful change to witness. As a facilitator – and a grown-up - I do have to be prepared to say the uncomfortable things that need to be said. Yet, I also need to hold back at times on those uncomfortable statements and allow others to do the hard work of speaking what's true.

> *"When we make a choice to share a genuine opinion with others, who also have their own unique point of view, we're entering territory that will inevitably have some rough and tumble."*

My field test had so far proven that paradox is, indeed, the missing ingredient to how the three principles of being a grown-up align to the work I do as a professional facilitator. Principle #1: The classes were not about me and they are also all about me. My example of being open and vulnerable paved the way for others to take the conversation to a deeper level. Principle #2: Be prepared to say the uncomfortable things and to also know when to keep quiet. The space we created in the workshop by not speaking gave others the opportunity to examine their actions and behavior and to own them.

The final lesson in refining my facilitation point of view came during my last leadership seminar in China.

Principle #3 of Robinson's characteristics of being a grown-up is the recognition that life is complex and tragic. Given my experience so far in seeing the paradox in principles one and two, I had already been reflecting on how paradox might play out in principle #3. If the existing principle is that life is complex and tragic, the paradox must be that life is also simple and blessed. That idea was easy to sign up for, but I was wondering how it would play out as I entered the complicated world of leadership development in China.

This was my first trip to China and my first time facilitating a group of high-level Chinese executives. While I knew the content well and had confidence in my ability to teach, I couldn't shake the overriding sense of worry. My concern was rooted in the complexity of the situation I was entering. It was the debut of this workshop in China. Though everyone there spoke English as a 2nd, 3rd or 4th language, there were real pressures and concerns about how the material would translate to this audience of Chinese national leaders. Plus, I knew that culturally the material might challenge their traditional view of leadership. My awareness of the complexity of the situation was definitely fully engaged.

However, by the end of day one, we had successfully traversed the language and translation challenges, course objectives, and most of the activities. I began to relax, believing that navigating this situation wouldn't be so difficult after all. But that confidence was about to be challenged.

When the session ended, a female leader from within the group approached me with a request. I assumed she was just another curious participant wanting to hear about my experiences living and working in the United States. However, her question was not about my life as an American. She wanted help with a difficult challenge she was facing in her new role as a leader within this software giant. On the one hand, I was glad she sought me out. On the other hand, I felt terrified at the prospect of coaching her. The complex nature of her unique situation caused me to doubt my ability. After all, what do I know about the life of a female technical leader in China? How could I possibly understand the intricacies of running a business in this country? How quickly would she figure out I would be of no use to her? Those were the thoughts running around in my head as we walked to a conference room after class.

Once we had privacy, she explained she had recently been appointed director of an emerging new business this organization was launching. Her thick accent made it difficult for me to fully understand her, even though I had just spent all day listening to her colleagues speak. Another complexity to manage. I began asking her specifics about the business, budgets, her colleagues, the technology – all of which she answered thoroughly - making me even more uncertain of how I could help. Then, to my surprise, she began telling me about her home life situation, something else difficult for me to relate to and, again, adding to the complexity of everything.

For a few seconds, I close my eyes and take a breath. And in a moment of clarity, I suddenly realize I haven't yet asked her what the specific problem was that she wanted to discuss. I ask her to describe to me the most significant challenge she is facing. Momentarily she hesitates. And that's when I notice she's fighting back tears. "I'm worried," she admits softly, "that very soon my leaders and the team will realize I am a fraud. When they see the real me, they will think I am not the right person for this promotion."

In an instant, all the complexities completely fade away. The beauty of her vulnerability and the humanity of her words show me as clear as day the paradox of principle #3: While I need to be aware of life's complexities, I also need to realize how simple life can be; because all this woman needs right now is someone to listen to her pain, reassure her that her feelings are normal, and help her believe in herself. Yes, Robinson was right: Life is certainly complicated. And it's also quite simple. When I'm overwhelmed with the complexities I see, I am best served to recall the foundation of my point of view: To live a life in community, nurturing my relationships with others. My field test is complete.

Our point of view is how we make sense of the world at any given moment. It's influenced by our beliefs, our experiences, our passions, and our purpose. We share our point of view with others so they know us and have a deeper insight into our intentions. We share what's in our minds, as a path to what's in our hearts. To thrive in change, we cannot lose ourselves. Resentment, anger and frustration often result, not through the actions of others, but through our abandonment of our point of view. Knowing and sharing your point of view are critical strategies in successfully navigating the rumble. And the paradox is there, too; in navigating the rumble, you may discover that your point of view changes.

Your Rumble Zone

In our community drum circle format, we ask each participant to improvise the beats they play. We don't usually teach structured rhythms that repeat for an hour. Instead, each drummer in the circle is invited to express themselves rhythmically in their own way, with their spirit fueling their musical imagination. Programs like HealthRhythms and Rhythm to Recovery use tested protocols to allow participants to express their emotions and internal thoughts, using the drum to amplify their words. Participants in a drum circle, in some form or other, are finding and expressing their point of view through the drum.

Finding and expressing one's point of view in a change or transition in life calls upon similar reflections to those when making up rhythms in a drum circle. What are the rhythms I have learned in the past? Which do I enjoy playing the most? How do I feel about what I'm hearing in the current groove? I have a beat to offer the groove, and I want to flow with the groove as I express my beat, not overwhelm it. I believe in the beat I want to share. It's a part of me. How can I express this rhythm and make the overall groove even more inclusive and dynamic by adding my point of view?

Reflections

It's often helpful to discover your point of view by learning from the points of view you already hold. Look back at the times in your life when you have successfully navigated a challenging and changing situation.

- Which of these do you have a strong point of view about?

- What motivates you to have this point of view?

- What past experiences informed your point of view?

After this reflection, determine three lessons you have learned (macro points of view) from the challenges you have faced.

Now, look back at the rumbles in your Rumble Zone and identify a particular situation you do not have a strong point of view about.

- Given the three macro points of view were so influential in your previous challenges, how could you apply them now? Keep what makes sense, throw out what doesn't. Your goal is at least 1 or 2 new points of view.

It's not just about having a point of view. To rumble is to then share the point of view with relevant others.

- Who is the person you feel most comfortable sharing this point of view with?

- Who would be the riskiest person to share your point of view with?

- To get where you want to go, who needs to hear this point of view?

Chapter 5

Get Curious

I have no particular talent. I am merely inquisitive.

–Albert Einstein

The ride on the ferry from the Bolivar Peninsula to Galveston Island was a joy for both of us. My mother stood beaming at the rail of the ferry boat, sun shining on her face, wind blowing through her hair. She loved the water and our impromptu adventure. I was happy to share this time with her.

But this excursion was going to be more than a day at the beach. It was the beginning of a new approach to relating to my mom and her needs as she aged. It had become very clear to my siblings and I that my mom's current living situation was not the best for her safety and quality of life. She no longer had the physical capability to keep up the house. And I realized that, despite all the sibling conversations, differing opinions, and complex family dynamics, I had spent virtually no time actually asking my mother what she herself wanted. I never asked her directly where she wanted to live as she grew older. Yet, that simple question was loaded with fear and sadness. But I knew I had to ask, and I knew I had to truly hear her answer. Of course, I had a strong point of view about where she should live. And to ask and listen to her perspective didn't negate my point of view at all. In fact, asking and listening gave me more information. I also knew I had to get beyond my own wall of fear and sadness to learn more. What were her fears? What was motivating her desire to stay in a home that she often told me she wanted out of? I needed to learn about her perspective. And I wanted to learn, not because I wanted to change her mind or mine - but just to learn. I needed to offer true curiosity.

When you're willing to rumble, you are willing to wrestle with different points of view. Sometimes those contrasting points of view are inside your own head. Sometimes, we are wrestling to understand the points of view of others. In either case, if you want to successfully lead through change, you need to be curious about these various points of views. In other words, to learn as an adult is to exercise true curiosity.

I work with successful business leaders every day. I see them navigating complex organizations, authoring detailed technical reports, crafting extraordinary strategic visions, nurturing new talent, and managing multiple high-profile stakeholders. To continue being successful, these leaders need to learn every moment. Not necessarily through traditional classrooms and teachers; they learn in the moment, through observation, prototyping, and most importantly, curiosity.

Types of Curiosity

To be curious about yourself and beyond yourself is a key strategy in the rumble. To be curious about yourself is a component of almost everything we've covered so far: Being curious requires courage, the ability to see and be present to what's happening in the moment, and to assess the situation against your own point of view. To be curious beyond yourself is to acknowledge you don't live in a vacuum and there's so much more to learn.

What do we get curious about? There is so much happening around us, every day, in every moment: ongoing interactions with others; a business market we operate within; the larger, complex natural world impacting us all the time. Learning in these areas offers continual opportunities to exercise curiosity beyond yourself. But always with the recognition that you are also part of this larger system.

We learn about the people around us in our lives. The people we want to be closer to, whom we want to nurture as a part of our family and community. What is the simplest and most effective way we can learn about them? Ask. When we are curious about our surroundings, we learn about nature, the place we live, the world around us. When we are curious about our situations, the everyday flow of events around us, we learn about the life we have helped create. We not only learn about others, but through others we learn about ourselves. To learn as an adult is to exercise true curiosity.

> "*If we keep our curiosity at a surface level, we miss half of the equation necessary for authentic transformation.*"

In the business world, we talk about feedback, coaching, and performance reviews. All those offer opportunities to get curious. We can immediately judge right and wrong, or we can take a learning stance; ask a few questions and recognize the world may not really be as it first appears. If we want to improve the quality of our conversations and relationships, curiosity will open new doors of wisdom and connection, providing us with many more choices.

Deeper Levels of Curiosity

Questions are one of the primary tools coaches use to help clients break through professional and personal barriers. Questions reveal context and ensure the coach and client are working from a similar set of data. Coaches are curiosity partners with their clients, helping the client reflect upon themselves. A client once described me as his alter ego, always challenging his current thinking.

As a coach, I utilize two types of curiosity. The information I glean from my client's inner life (curiosity about the self) and the data I collect about the situations my client is currently working through (curiosity beyond the self).

Each of these types of curiosity offers deeper levels to explore. Fact-based curiosity is related to what, how, and when. Heart-based curiosity is related to what, why, and wonder.

Fact-Based Curiosity

Fact-based curiosity is necessary to learn the data regarding what has happened in any given situation. We're curious about what happened and what was the triggering event, how it happened, when the process started, what steps one took. All of this provides us with important data about the events. The word "fact" here indicates this is curiosity focused on what can be seen, heard, or tangibly touched.

You might think of fact-based curiosity as inquiry and dialog about what you see. Imagine for a moment you are on a boat, churning past icebergs in the North Atlantic Sea. As you see the iceberg from your view above the water, you see a portion of the iceberg. Fact-based curiosity is focused on what you can see as you pass the iceberg: the number of jagged edges, how much it rises above the seawater, the color of the ice. In the same way, when we are curious about others, we often start our inquiry with what we have seen of them: the projects they are working on, the behaviors they exhibit, the words they speak. That's how others present themselves to the world, just as the top of the iceberg is how it presents itself to a passing ship.

However, just because the ship only sees a portion of the iceberg above the water doesn't mean the tip of the iceberg is the only thing the ship needs to be concerned about. Most of the iceberg doesn't show up above the water. It extends well beyond what we see above the water into the depths of the ocean. In the same way, what we see and hear of others (their behaviors, actions, and words) are only a small part of who they are as a person. Ships have sonar and maps to help navigate what can't be seen from above the waterline. In the same way, as human beings, we need to dive more deeply into ourselves and others if we want a more accurate picture and understanding of any person or situation. If we want to truly know other people, who they are and what influences their beliefs and behaviors, we need to explore beneath the waterline, past the facts that we can see, into the depth of their human experience: their emotions, thoughts, and judgments. For this, we need to pursue heart-based curiosity.

Heart-Based Curiosity

All human beings are metaphorically like that iceberg. There is so much more than what we see on the surface. To be able to authentically connect with someone, we need to look beyond the obvious. It is there, in the depths of the human soul, where true connection can occur. We must go there if we are willing to rumble. Heart-based curiosity creates the opportunity for genuine relationships and learning beyond the events happening or plans being made. People are often hungry for someone to ask the heart-based questions, but they rarely have the courage to ask you to do that.

Teaching leaders to apply coaching practices in their management style is a good illustration of how Fact-Based questions differ in impact from Heart-Based questions.

As a certified professional coach, I have been trained to go beyond the surface by asking the deeper questions. It's a critical skill to learn when teaching coaching to others. In one class, I was teaching coaching skills to medical professionals who served as leaders in a prestigious medical system. We were practicing coaching techniques in a group setting, with one student coaching another student while the other students observed. Each student in turn would have an opportunity to serve as a coach and be observed by their colleagues. One of the clients being coached laid out two potential dilemmas she wanted to discuss in her coaching conversation. One was work-related and the other home-related, but both very valid situations to discuss with a coach. After the client laid out the scenarios, the student coach suggested they begin with the work dilemma first. That began a series of informative exchanges between the coach and client, covering various areas of her work. The student coach exercised curiosity by asking and learning a great deal about the client's professional situation. All this information was informative, relevant, and factual. The goal of the conversation was to see if the client could gain some insight into the difficulties she was facing. They identified many systemic challenges that could be explored further, but as I watched the interaction, I could sense that the issue being discussed was not the heart of the issue.

After ten minutes of coaching, I offered a different student the opportunity to sit in the coach's chair with the same person as the client. This second coach, a woman, immediately asked the client which of the two dilemma scenarios she would have preferred to talk about – work or home, allowing the client to choose. The client said she would have preferred discussing her home life first. The second coach demonstrated true curiosity by setting aside her own assumptions and genuinely inviting the client's point of view.

That deeper question led to a series of personal revelations about the challenge of work/life balance, which as is turned out, was the root cause of the work challenge the client had discussed earlier. She revealed the emotional conflict between her priorities at work and a changing family life at home. She needed to open up emotionally, release tension, and share the roadblock that was stopping her from taking the next steps. Through this deeper connection with the second coach, the client was able to take a fresh look at her professional and personal life. Heart-based curiosity often leads to these deeper levels of connection and awareness and can uncover insights necessary to thrive in the rumble.

> *"Unconscious confirmation bias is a great danger to true curiosity."*

There's an on-going joke I often hear when teaching others coaching skills. At some point during the coaching conversation, I will ask my client "How do you feel about...?" seeking to connect with them below the surface at the heart level. This "How do you feel about...?" question is often responded to with skeptical commentary like, "Oh, there it is, the feeling question." This response may be a deflection to avoid going deeper into their motivation and feeling. We joke about the feeling question, but in reality, the joke is an avoidance mechanism. So, I tend to disregard it and ask again, "Well, how do you feel about it?"

Other times, when I ask that heart-based question, the reply will start with "Well, I feel that...." Some interesting thoughts might be uncovered as the person continues speaking, but more than likely it won't reveal an emotion. Statements starting with "I feel that..." are usually followed with thoughts related to personal judgments. While those are all potentially interesting points of view, they may not lead to the heart. Heart-based curiosity ideally should help the other person connect to their feelings. I might need to initially ask, "Do you feel good or bad about the situation you described?" This question becomes a first step into the heart by offering options on how the other might feel, as opposed to asking the fully opened-ended question, "How do you feel about...?"

When we ask others heart-based questions, we are inviting them to share from deep within their internal experience. We are asking them to be curious about themselves.

Heart-based curiosity of self is a powerful tool that helps the person learn about their own emotions, whether they are emotions directed inward or outward. We are either expressing curiosity to learn more about our own circumstances or we're expressing curiosity to help others learn about themselves and their circumstances.

Confirmation Bias: An Insidious Block to True Curiosity

Webster's defines curiosity as "a strong desire to learn or know something." Up to this point, we have looked at types of curiosity that help fulfill this desire to learn something new. However, in the pursuit of true curiosity, we must consider if our curiosity is shaded by an insidious and potentially unconscious detractor, known as confirmation bias.

Confirmation bias, as defined by Webster is "the tendency to search for, interpret, favor, and recall information in a way that confirms one's pre-existing beliefs or hypotheses." This tendency, as referenced in the definition, is something we're both aware of and unaware of; something that can be either helpful or limiting. Confirmation bias causes us to look for data that confirms what we already believe. Here are a few examples:

As a man, one of the key indicators that tells me I'm in the men's public bathroom at the airport (other than the sign on the door or the men walking in) is that I see urinals inside. Recently, I was leading a workshop at a large conference center. The workshop sponsor told me that he walked into the bathroom, didn't see urinals, and assumed he had walked into the women's room by mistake. So, he walked out, looked at the sign, which read Men's Room. However, based on his bias from past experiences, he thought the sign was incorrect. He was looking for his specific expectation to be met to confirm where he was and did not trust the sign on the wall.

Confirmation bias also shows up frequently in politics. Not long ago, I was participating in a political discussion with some colleagues.

Since I knew where most of them stood on issues, the content of the conversation was not of much interest to me. What became obvious was that many of those aligned with a specific party or ideology would reference news articles, commentators, and media preferences that were of their same belief or ideology. (Republicans and conservatives referenced Fox News, The Wall Street Journal, and The National Review; Democrats and progressives referenced MSNBC, The New York Times, and The Nation.) We can easily create a news stream that appeals to our beliefs. That news isn't news; it's a way to confirm points of view about what we already think.

Now, consider how confirmation bias impacts curiosity. We want to be curious, to ask questions, to learn about a person or a situation. The inherent nature of confirmation bias tells us we listen and interpret information to fit into our point of view. This is how we learn. We hear from others, contrast against what we know, and then decide if what the other has said is something we want to retain, or something irrelevant that we want to forget. Our tendency is to look first for data that confirms our belief about the person or situation.

This happens often in my work in facilitating leadership development workshops. Recently, I was leading a workshop for a large technology firm in a room of experienced leaders at senior levels of the organization. We were discussing coaching and improving the performance of others. The class indicated this was a topic they had prioritized for their development because they were having a challenge retaining top talent. They knew who I was, my level of expertise, and my experience studying coaching and behavioral science. As I shared important coaching information and skills, a set of individuals in the room continued to reject most of the teaching. Over and over, they looked for reasons why it wouldn't work in their group. They came into the room having already decided coaching would fail - but most were not aware of their bias. Even though my teaching and this coaching model were completely new to them, they were determined to find how it couldn't possibly be a match for their needs.

This is not an isolated event in my workshops. Yet it's not all about confirmation bias. There are various leadership styles, organizational factors, and other circumstances that influenced these leaders. One of these influencing factors was confirmation bias.

The saddest outcome of all of this is that when these leaders left the room, they'd confirmed their own belief - that coaching would not work - even though that's what they asked for in the first place. They defended their stance by reiterating they were certainly open to learning but the material presented just missed the mark. I would argue that their unconscious confirmation bias looked for reasons in my content to confirm their own judgments, rather than being open to learning something new.

Unconscious confirmation bias is a great danger to true curiosity. Why? Because its insidious nature leads us to believe that we've been curious and open to taking in new information; that we've exercised the behaviors of curiosity - asking questions. However, when we asked those questions, did we hear what the other truly said, or did we hear our interpreted (and potentially biased) version of what they said? Did we seek out sources of information aligned with our beliefs to confirm what we already knew and to reject outside points of view? In the end, were we aware at all of possible confirmation bias?

Two Paths of True Curiosity: Depth and Breadth

Fact-based curiosity helps us learn more about what we see (like the portion of the iceberg above the water). Heart-based curiosity helps us understand what we cannot see - the emotions, beliefs, and mindsets often unobservable in others, but just below the surface (like the portion of the iceberg beneath the water). When we exercise true curiosity, we are drilling down into the depths of something specific - exploring ourselves, another person, or a situation. However, sometimes this deeper curiosity leads us to surprising or fresh information that can shift the topic to a brand new set of behaviors, circumstances, or people. When this happens, we have increased the breadth of what we know about a situation. Our curiosity is no longer drilling downward but now side-stepping to something else (a new iceberg, with a new set of visible behaviors).

A clear example of this type of breadth curiosity occurred when I was hired by a family foundation to coach a senior executive. This executive was leading an initiative for clean drinking water and improved sanitation in remote countries. The coaching was specifically to address this leader's verbally abusive and disruptive management style. The leader had been observed exhibiting behaviors of yelling, using foul language, and creating a toxic environment for his team. What complicated the situation was that this executive also had a great deal of expertise with this initiative, as well as with the organization's mission. I was brought in to work with him in an effort to turn around his destructive approach to leadership.

At the beginning of our coaching engagement, I exercised a great deal of curiosity, asking him many questions about the abusive circumstances and his choices as a leader. I was using Fact-Based Curiosity to learn more about the behaviors others had seen. While we were talking about some of the incidents, I looked for opportunities to move my curiosity from the facts to the heart. At one point, he discussed frustration and ultimately disappointment with his own behaviors. I used this as an opportunity to dive deeper into those feelings by asking him to tell me more about his frustration. I made the choice to move beyond his actions into his motivation and emotion. This choice to get curious about the depth of the person is a choice for heart-based curiosity. While that was the path I chose, I could have just as easily continued with fact-based, situational questions about the story and circumstances. However, if we keep our curiosity at a surface level, we miss half of the equation necessary for authentic transformation. As he began talking more honestly about the disappointment he felt, we were able to get past the circumstances of the situation and discover an important experience from his past that was contributing to his emotions today. The past situation was another "iceberg" of circumstances and feelings.

Going deeper into his situation revealed facts and emotions from the past that were still impacting his choices today. This expanded our understanding of his current situation. It wasn't just about this present day challenge, but also about the lingering impact of a challenge from his past.

Curiosity leads us to more information to get curious about, not only by drilling down into the depth of a person or situation, but also by stepping across to expand the breadth of what we're learning. Expanding the depth and breadth of our knowledge through curiosity always helps us understand people and situations better. And that awareness is exactly what we need to successfully navigate the rumble. When we go beneath the surface of people, situations, processes and other factors, we can uncover how we are being impacted in conscious and unconscious ways. Getting curious gives us access to the systemic factors that are blocking, pushing, or influencing the current situation in some way.

> "*Getting curious gives us access to the systemic factors that are blocking or influencing the current situation in some way.*"

This is exactly what happened with my coaching sessions at the family foundation. We found that these systemic factors relating to the executive's past experiences were absolutely influencing the choices he made working with his team. His challenging past was directly influencing choices in the present. Once we had this awareness, we were able to talk though a new approach to leadership. He gained a renewed sense of relief from knowing there were past circumstances impacting his decisions today. With this new knowledge, he felt empowered to do something different to re-establish his role as an effective leader.

But does true curiosity ever end? How do we know when we've gone deep enough or expanded broadly enough to get all the information we need, yet not too deep or so broad that we're wasting time? We don't want to fall into the trap of analysis paralysis - asking so many questions that we sacrifice action for curiosity. This is where the art of curiosity lies. Just as with all these strategies, too much of anything can take you farther away from transformation. If we keep our intention focused, remain connected to the other, and stay mindful in the moment, we can use curiosity to gain valuable information and demonstrate willingness to learn in the rumble.

Your Rumble Zone

Any time a drum circle facilitator enters the circle to change the groove, we see the results of their intention in their body language and words. We don't see the layers upon layers of thoughts, emotions, training, beliefs or experiences leading to that intention. This is true for all the drummers in the circle, too. We see them playing, but don't know the judgmental thoughts, self-doubt, joy or frustrations they may feel inside. We don't know their backgrounds, values, or intentions, we just see the tip of their iceberg. The musical dialog becomes the expression of the underneath of the iceberg. Outside of the drum circle, curiosity can help turn the musical dialog into shared insights.

Reflections

To best develop curiosity towards others, we must practice curiosity towards ourselves. Being willing to rumble means going beyond the surface of the iceberg, past our superficial nature and into the depths of what it means to be a person, a member, or a leader.

Consider the immediate thoughts from your Rumble Zone as the tip of an iceberg. Everything you know about the situation is seen, above the water, from your perspective. But there are volumes of information below the waterline, not known unless offered or asked about. To be willing to rumble is to be willing to ask questions below the waterline. Some questions helpful to explore below the waterline include:

- What previous circumstances have contributed to the current challenge?

- How are the working relationships between you and others involved?

- What beliefs or values are you supporting with your actions? Do these feel authentic to you?

- What is your intention in this scenario? What do you know about the intentions of others?

Your iceberg is only one of many floating around. Now that you've done the work of getting curious about yourself, it's time to extend your curiosity to others.

- Who are key individuals affected?
- What can you learn from them to expand your point of view?

Each of those individuals has their own iceberg with their own stories of themselves and others. You know what's in your iceberg. Share your perspective to balance your curiosity about their perspectives. Ask them the same questions you asked yourself.

Chapter 6

Strive for Empathy

> Empathy is about finding echoes
> of another person in yourself.
>
> –Mohsin Hamid

One of my greatest strengths as a facilitator is an ability to express empathy. Clients give me that feedback frequently. Yet it's often the case that one's strengths, when overused, can become a weakness. So, it's not surprising that one of the most painful pieces of feedback I ever heard was about my overuse of empathy.

    Something happened in a workshop I was facilitating triggering a lot of anger in me towards a colleague. At the time, I couldn't acknowledge my own feelings. Instead, I continued to return to an empathetic stance, imagining how hard the situation must be for my colleague. Eventually, a close friend challenged me to set aside this empathetic stance and look more deeply at my own emotions. The truth was, I felt wounded and betrayed. In my attempt to be empathetic toward someone else, I was leaving myself behind. While empathy can be a great asset, like any skill, it can also be overused. Until I acknowledged my own emotional state, it would be next to impossible to repair the relationship with my colleague. Once I showed myself empathy, my colleague and I were able to connect more deeply. Striving for empathy - toward others as well as ourselves - is critical in successfully navigating the rumble of change.

    There is a drive within most of us to be in a relationship with others; we are inherently social beings. The other people in our lives continually observe our patterns of behaviors and attitudes. They come to rely on us, especially those closest to us, just as we rely on them. As we begin to count on the behaviors and attitudes of others, we form expectations of how the other should be, just as others have expectations of how we should be towards them. We have developed a pattern in how we relate to others and a pattern of how we expect others to relate to us.

Inevitably, changes occur. These changes range from the simple to complex. We decide to change our diet and become a vegan. While we are making a personal change to our eating habits, this change could potentially impact others. Consider the work colleague who you have eaten lunch with for the past few years. The two of you have developed a pattern of where to eat and how to share the time at lunch together. And now you are changing the pattern to improve your health by shifting the choices you make for food. While this is your choice, your social contract with your work colleague is now thrown out of balance as she catches up with your new choice. Her response to your choice could range from curiosity to indifference to frustration. And how she chooses to respond could contribute to your successfully making the change or it could hinder your ability to successfully make the change you want to make.

Your will to do something different initiates the rumble state. But this change is not occurring in a vacuum. You are changing the terms of your unwritten social contract with others and, like it or not, their responses are relevant to your ability to sustain your new path.

To thrive in the rumble means considering the impact of change on the others in our life.

Having an empathetic attitude helps us anticipate the emotional reactions the other might have to our change. If we can put ourselves in their shoes and accept their reactions, we're better equipped to withstand their response. Will you show grace or defensiveness? Will you over- explain to justify your point of view, rather than just listening? Do you have the resilience to endure their reaction and stay true to the vision you have for your new pathway?

There are 3 primary blocks to striving for empathy:

1. Misunderstanding empathy

2. Being consumed with our own agenda

3. Resentment because of another's repeated poor behavior

Misunderstanding Empathy

Empathy is the act of striving to understand the feelings of another. It is not passing judgment on whether their feelings are justified. When you express empathy, you are not showing sympathy. Sympathy implies a sense of sorrow or pity for the other – empathy does not. Empathy does not imply that they are right and you are wrong. You can express empathy without agreeing or feeling the exact same feeling. Empathy is accepting the other feels the way they feel. When we are empathetic, we are not trying to talk the person out of feeling what they feel. We are, instead, witnessing their true current state.

In the context of a rumble, we must also be aware our effort to change ourselves may trigger emotion in others. While their response may be triggered by our choice, we didn't create the trigger in the other person; it's their trigger to manage. They were set off by a change in behavior we are attempting to make. When we are empathic to them being triggered, we are not taking responsibility for their behaviors or words as they work through their trigger. Empathy is accepting their current state is real and true. Empathically, we recognize we contributed to the situation by expressing our want, but we did not cause it.

Consumed with Our Own Agenda

When we fail to express empathy, one of the primary causes of failure is our consumption with our own agenda. Our own point of view and emotions can block our ability to consider the impact of what we're saying.

A clear example of this occurred with a colleague whom I have deep respect for. Carolyn and I met as trainers for a software company. We both shared a passion for excellence. When I stepped down as Director of Facilitation, she took over my role.

Her first responsibility was planning a worldwide trainers conference. This conference was a big investment for the company. We were originally going to have this conference two years earlier. I had been the lead designer and host for the original conference. I had researched venues, built a staff to handle the logistics, and completed the design of the conference. I was excited. However, as happens in business, an economic downturn caused management to cancel the conference.

While I understood the business decision from a logical perspective, I felt hurt and frustrated with the decision. I knew the decision wasn't personal, but I allowed it to affect me personally. I felt our training division was being disrespected in the decision. I was personally disappointed I was not going to host this worldwide gathering. I wanted the experience of being the conference host. Now, two years later, we were offered another opportunity to bring the staff together, but I was no longer the lead for the conference. Carolyn had that role.

I was very happy when Carolyn asked me to co-lead the design and hosting of the conference. I met with her on our first day of planning and she shared the budget and venues for this rescheduled event. The budget and plans were scaled back to less than half of what we had been allocated for the previous conference. Given this limited budget, it became clear that my original vision for the conference was not going to happen.

As we reviewed the numbers, I became more frustrated and discouraged. With a much smaller venue, shorter conference, and such a limited budget, I felt disrespected again. Consumed with negative emotions towards the leaders and the organization, I was completely unaware how my anger was affecting Carolyn. She came into this opportunity excited about the potential of the conference. While the plans were being scaled back, for her it was still a momentous event being given to us by the leadership. In addition, it was her first high-profile event to design in her new role. I was blind to her excitement, consumed by my own petty frustrations that we were not getting what we originally had been allocated.

> "*Your will to do something different initiates the rumble state. You are changing the terms of your unwritten social contract with others and, like it or not, their responses are relevant to your ability to sustain your new path.*"

I gave into my own immaturity and emotion, "This whole thing is a waste of time," I told her. I can still remember the hurt look on her face. My dismissive comment derailed our work session and showed my lack of will to make the most out of the situation. Instead of being willing to rumble and figure out the path to the new conference, I sabotaged the moment. Being consumed with my own agenda caused me to overlook the human being in front of me.

Thankfully, we got back on track. I was able to repair the relationship. We held a spectacular conference. But, to this day, it was a painful lesson for me. My own agenda undermined my ability to show Carolyn empathy. From that, I've learned to step back and pause if I'm having an intense emotional reaction to a situation. I now manage those emotions so I can stay connected to the other person. In the middle of the rumble, I want to show them empathy and focus on nurturing the relationship.

Resentment Due to Repeated Patterns of Behavior

Another barrier to striving for empathy can be the emotional scar tissue in place from years of repeated patterns of hurtful behavior from another. It is incredibly difficult to muster empathy for another person if past experiences with the person have driven a wedge between the two of you. Regardless of the change or situation either is pursuing, once that wedge is in place, showing empathy can be next to impossible. If we are feeling discouraged, struggling to let go of old patterns in our relationships, showing empathy can be the last thing on our mind. And yet, that lack of empathy can inhibit our change efforts, push us back into old, ineffective patterns and farther away from where we ultimately want to be.

A deeply personal example revolves around my relationship with my father, who was a very serious alcoholic. His drinking was a part of everything we did. Watching television – get dad a beer. Working on televisions at his workplace – get dad a beer. Deer hunting, driving, cooking – get dad a beer. As I grew into a teenager, I became more and more ambivalent about him. In my mother's attempts to get him to quit drinking, we tried Alcoholics Anonymous, 12 steps, outpatient recovery centers, inpatient recovery centers, shock treatment, and a host of other strategies. We all tried to help him shift the pattern of behavior that was toxic to him and those he loved. But he did not have the will to stop drinking – he was not willing to rumble with the struggle of overcoming addiction.

When my mother finally decided to divorce him, I found myself unable to find any reason at all to stay connected with him. My father had seen his business fail, his marriage fall apart, his health decline, and his connection to friends, family, and community rot on the vine. In all his pain, I was unable to find any empathy or understanding for him. There were too many past scars to overcome to find the place in my heart where I could begin to imagine what he was feeling. The impact of his past behaviors became an obstacle to expressing empathy for him I could not overcome.

After the divorce, I saw him only a handful of times. When he suffered a massive stroke, I decided to visit him in the hospital, even though he was in a comatose state, unaware of my presence. I talked to him about the past, about my regrets, about my confusion and sadness. It was all about me. Even at his death bed, I could not access any empathy for his life. He died a few days later. I remained in this frozen, ambivalent, and apathetic state towards him for years.

It wasn't until an assignment in graduate school that everything changed. We were instructed to engage in truthful, vulnerable conversations with members of our family. If they were deceased, we were supposed to go to their grave and spend time in self-reflection.

"When we are empathetic, we are not trying to talk the person out of feeling what they feel. We are instead witnessing their true current state."

I'll never forget the experience of seeing my father's gravestone. I'm named after him. It was a surreal experience sitting at a grave with my own name on it. I struggled with how to begin this one-sided conversation. I used the homework assignment questions from the class. As I read the questions, I realized I had no idea how my father would have responded to any of them. I never really knew him. What was the internal drive that caused him to value drinking more than his family? What event in his life led him to believe that he couldn't overcome his alcoholism? What was his favorite color? I didn't know anything about him. I felt a deep sadness, but not for me. For him. I couldn't imagine what events had happened in his life that led him to make the choices he made – choices that caused so much pain for others – and for himself. Before I knew it, the questions became a salve on my heart. I felt an opening. A new curiosity towards him. What burdens did he carry? What was it like for him to feel he had no support? I felt deeply grateful for my own loving friends and community. And, in seeing and accepting the huge burden he carried, I started to feel true empathy towards him.

Scar tissues preventing us from showing empathy can run deep. They can be a barrier getting us stuck in a rumble state, rather than using the rumble as a bridge to a new pathway. But, in finding a way to show empathy, I released my desire for the past to be different. It was no longer about my past; it was about his. In my lack of knowledge of his background, I found a doorway to begin understanding how he must have felt.

How can we strive for empathy for the other, recognizing they too are navigating a rumble, perhaps triggered by our actions? While we are not responsible for their reactions, we can anticipate them. Imagine you were hearing the news you just shared with them for the first time. How would you react? Wouldn't you want them to show empathy for you? We don't have to agree with or like someone's response, but we can manage ourselves in a way that supports them and doesn't make things worse. Striving for empathy can give us the opportunity to allow them to catch up with our new point of view. In the end, it can bring us closer and deepen our connection. And that's one of the great benefits of being willing to rumble.

Your Rumble Zone

A classic example of how a facilitator interacts with a drum circle is a call and response. The facilitator plays a 4-beat pattern, the call. The group of novice drummers repeats the pattern as best they can, the response. That simple act is a starting place for empathy. One person shares, the others listen and respond with the same pattern; an acknowledgement of their hearing the message. Sometimes, the facilitator will surprise a drummer in the circle by delegating the call to an unsuspecting drummer. Everyone has to respond to the drummer's pattern, regardless of what it is. The goal is to repeat whatever the drummer's call sounds like, even if the participant is so shocked by being selected that he laughs or shouts instead of playing his drum. The drummers learn that others have responses that are similar and different to their own. Self-awareness and awareness of others increases with the call and responses, to create relationships between the drummers. The drummers are sharing rhythms, repeating rhythms, and seeing each other as individuals, as well as a group. The relationship between the members is strengthened. These types of activities lead us toward empathy.

Reflections

==Empathy starts with listening==; the kind of listening that allows the speaker to know we are engaged with them. One way to do that is to listen without being distracted by devices or our own agendas. When listening, show interest with eye contact and verbal cues. Another way to show true engagement in the conversation is to actively listen by repeating your understanding of what has been said or asking questions relevant to the speaker's topic. In this exchange of sharing and hearing, a relationship develops. We have more information about the thoughts and feelings of the other person. We see that our thoughts and feelings may be the same or they may be different. Our self-awareness increases.

In the growth of our own self-awareness, along with the developing awareness of the other, we see the contrast between us. This contrast becomes the distraction that takes us away from being empathic. ==Instead of letting the contrast be, we want to decrease the contrast by offering advice or passing== judgment. An empathetic stance does none of that. Instead, expressing empathy is acknowledging the other's perspective and the contrast between us. Empathy acknowledges that their perspective is just as true and real to them as our perspective is as true and real to us.

Look back at your Rumble Zone.

- Where are the instances you may have been more judgmental towards another rather than empathetic?
- How might your judgments of others be contributing to the disturbance you are experiencing in this rumble?

- Who are the individuals you could seek out and listen to with the intention of building a relationship? Not a best friend, but someone with whom you can give a moment of acceptance for who they are and what they are feeling.

Extending empathy to another may be the next step you need as you navigate the rumble.

Chapter 7

Bring an Open Mind

> Humility is the wisdom of accepting the truth that you might just be wrong.
>
> –Richard Paul Evans

This was my third time facilitating an Emotional Intelligence workshop for veterans from the wars in Afghanistan and Iraq. When I was first invited to be on the faculty of this Wounded Warriors program, I was reminded of all the past conversations and judgments I had encountered about war. Was going to war the right decision or wrong one? Did we succeed or fail? Were politics or national security the priority? I remembered the polarizing debates with friends and colleagues. Regardless of those judgments, I had to bring an open mind to this class. I was here to support these women and men as they learned to transition from a war mindset to a work mindset. How did they navigate the everyday concerns in the workplace with the wounds, both physical and mental, left by their service? While I knew nothing of the horrors of war, I knew how to listen and empathize. I also knew that understanding Emotional Intelligence could positively and profoundly impact one's ability to cope in a rumble. And I was passionate about sharing this knowledge with these veterans.

The workshop was sponsored by one of my corporate leadership development clients. This company created a 10-week professional development training program to help veterans gain the skills to assist their transition into the workplace. In the first cohort, I was initially given only 2 hours of curriculum time for the Emotional Intelligence session. That's because the sponsor was concerned that content labeled Emotional Intelligence would be perceived as too soft or irrelevant for this group. There was a real concern about the veterans' willingness to connect with the emotional nature of the work. However, our experience quickly proved otherwise.

I had just taught a section on the biology of the brain and the source of emotion. Emotions come from the limbic system in the brain. Our limbic system responds to an external stimulus micro-seconds before our prefrontal cortex responds with logical thought. In other words, we feel before we think. A key part of Emotional Intelligence is training ourselves to notice our emotional reaction before acting out unintentionally from the emotional response. Our thoughts can notice the emotion, help us to pause, take a breath, and choose the next action intentionally. If you've ever said something out of anger that you later regretted, then you've had the experience of acting out unintentionally based on an emotion. Cultivating that emotional awareness helps us bring an open mind to any situation.

One of the young men in the room, a veteran named John, raised his hand to share an insight. Up to this point of the workshop, John had appeared nervous and generally disengaged from the content. However, this time, he shared with the group that at different points in the workshop he could feel his rage building. Sometimes triggered by questions, sometimes by loud noises, and sometimes by almost nothing. He explained that his rage would swell; that he could feel it growing, like a train barreling down the tracks. "But I never knew I could make a different choice," he admitted. "I never realized that I could do something other than act out physically."

Before John shared this, I had been grappling with my own sense of despair about his silence, thinking the information was not getting through to him. But after hearing his insight, I was able to let go of my judgments and have a more open mind about the impact of the curriculum. I believed John now knew he could make a different choice. I witnessed his growth and I chose to judge my work as successful.

The reason it's important to bring an open mind to any situation is because we have no idea how the situation will ultimately turn out. Our brains are story-making machines. This can be helpful in many circumstances; however, we often make up a worse story than the actual outcome. And, just as unconscious bias can undermine curiosity, our stories or judgments can limit the possibilities in any new situation.

Because of the success with John, I was able to increase the number of hours for each additional cohort. The last session would be a full half-day of Emotional Intelligence curriculum. I was feeling confident in the work and proud of my opportunity to serve these women and men.

The third group of Wounded Warriors was the largest: thirty-two men and women from diverse backgrounds, races and religions, with a shared experience of war; each needing to integrate their identity as a veteran with that of a budding professional worker. I was humbled in the presence of their sacrifice and believed this would be some of the most important work I could ever do.

Bringing an open mind when learning Emotional Intelligence can be challenging for many people. Emotional Intelligence, also known as EQ, often calls us to confront the stories we've made up about how things work in our relationships and in ourselves.

Michael came to the third cohort with his story locked and loaded. During his service as a Marine, he served 2 tours of duty in Iraq, the second a much bloodier and deadlier experience than the first. I learned all this in class as Michael shared his personal narrative, along with his bold defiance of the curriculum.

Like all the classes before, I began teaching the basic biology of the brain. The limbic system is the first brain component engaged in response to events around us. These emotional responses provide information about what's happening. Like the thoughts that follow, these emotions are internal clues to help us make the best decisions and choices we can about what to do next. These are simple biological facts. But Michael passionately disagreed. He described in detail his experience as a Marine. He had no choice but to kill. He had no choice about seeing his best friend shot in front of him; about putting his Marine brothers in body bags. He insisted that he had conditioned himself to have absolutely no emotions about this; that there was no helpful information he was receiving inwardly. He emphasized that, as a Marine, he had a job to do, he was trained to do, and he did it. He let the group know his battlefield experience invalidated any research on the subject, biology or otherwise.

I had experienced push-back on this content before. I also had a deep trust in my facilitating and teaching skills to build a bridge between where Michael was and where I believed he could be. I acknowledged Michael's doubt and listened empathetically to his stories. My intention was not to invalidate his point of view but to accept him where he was, while continuing to believe that I could broaden his understanding. After a great deal of back and forth between Michael and me, it seemed best to pause our conversation, and focus on the full group. As a facilitator, responsible for all thirty-two participants, I suggested we move on and asked Michael to keep his mind open to the remaining content. I invited him to simply notice his questions and doubts. While Michael agreed to continue with an open mind, his behavior throughout the remainder of the class proved otherwise. He became my Doubting Thomas.

For the remaining hours of the workshop, Michael had a contrary and combative response to almost every topic in the curriculum. As the class proceeded, Michael became not only a passionate and enthusiastic critic of Emotional Intelligence, but also the embodiment of every Doubting Thomas I had ever encountered in all my past workshops. From the Ivy League graduate at General Electric who trivialized leadership development, to the tech genius entrepreneur who judged Emotional Intelligence as a waste of time, I began to feel the room crowd with past voices of dissent. That discord triggered my own feelings of inadequacy. I began shutting down on the inside from years of disagreement I had received from others. My ability to bring an open mind to the class was shrinking, along with my confidence in the work. And yet, ironically, those critical voices were all in my head. In this room, in this workshop, right now, it was only Michael.

Despite that truth, something inside of me decided I had finally met my match. In an instant, I closed my mind. I passed judgment on Michael. I chose to believe he didn't get it and that he would never get it. In passing this judgment, I gave up on my belief in the curriculum, the process, and my own abilities. Michael seemed to prove to me that there are limits to my effectiveness as a leadership coach and facilitator. After the workshop, I saw Michael speaking with a small group of his peers and reiterating his belief in the fallacy of Emotional Intelligence. I felt deeply misunderstood. Leaning over to the client sponsor, who was also observing Michael talking to his peers, I said, "Well, we can't reach everybody and clearly I didn't reach Michael." In fact, I wrote Michael off, labelling my work and its value for Michael as a waste of time. I felt physically heavy, as if a wet blanket had been thrown on top of me.

My thoughts centered around this failure. Like so many of my coaching clients, I found myself giving little value to all the successes in my career. Instead, I focused on my failure to reach Michael; and on his inability to be open to new data and possibilities. I didn't realize it then, but it was actually my own inability to stay open to new data and possibilities about Michael that was bringing this heaviness. As much as he had judged the class a total waste of time, I judged him as someone who would never ever get it.

> *"Our brains are story-making machines and we often make up a worse story than the actual outcome."*

In the weeks that followed, I continued with my regular work with organizational leaders, away from the intensity of the Wounded Warriors. As always, I encountered a wide range of workshop participants, from those eager to learn to those uninterested and defiant. I responded as I always did to the reluctant learner, with dignity and respect, intent on not giving up on the curriculum. But suddenly, all my skills and tools felt a little harder for me to access. I felt burdened by failure and doubt. The judgment I passed on Michael was seriously weighing me down. The moment I gave in and believed in his inability to ever understand Emotional Intelligence, my faith in the work itself diminished, along with my ability to bring an open mind to other situations. Deciding I had failed with Michael made transformation seem less possible with others. I was wilting under the weight of my own judgments. I decided I had to learn to operate in this new, self-imposed, limiting normal; a "normal" based on a decision I had made about another person. And this, at its core, identifies the challenge we face when we don't cultivate an open mind. We can use our knowledge and judgments of past experiences to evaluate current possibilities. But what if those judgments are made and acted on too quickly?

The Gift and Hindrance of Judgments

Human beings are inherently judgmental. Judgments keep us safe ("I think this may be too hot to touch"); judgments make us successful ("I think this product will be a winner"); judgments make us happy ("I'm going to like ice cream more than vinegar"). It's not bad that we're judgmental. But sometimes, for good reason at the time, we make limiting judgments. These judgments can weigh us down, cloud our view, and cause us to make poor decisions on the current event before it even happens. We set ourselves up for failure and unmet expectations.

To thrive in the rumble, one has to be willing to cultivate an open mind; to suspend judgments carried over from the past; in particular, those limiting ideas that say something will never work or a person will never change. If we cannot become aware of those limiting judgments, then today's path to success will be undermined by yesterday's perception of failure.

The judgments that tend to limit us the most are the judgments we have of others and of ourselves. This shows up often when adults come together in a group to discuss an important topic. At the beginning of every workshop I facilitate, I ask the group what they need from me and from each other to get the most out of our time together. Invariably, someone says, "I want us to have a non-judgmental environment." When I ask what they mean by "non-judgmental" they explain they want an environment where they can try something new or ask a question and not be judged if they don't do things right. In response, I often remind the participant that the most important place they'll want to establish that open-minded environment is inside their own heads; often, the worst judgments come from within.

> *"If we cannot become aware of our limiting judgments, then today's path to success will be undermined by yesterday's perception of failure."*

Yet, having a fully non-judgmental environment is not possible. We could certainly try asking everyone to keep an open mind, but that's easier said than done. So, how do we begin to cultivate an authentic stance of open-mindedness? The first step always begins with exercising willingness and awareness. We must be willing to consider the possibility of our own judgmentalism – we need to become aware of what we're thinking and feeling. And if we can do that, we can continue taking in new information and allow our judgments to evolve.

My experience with Michael is a perfect illustration of the dangers of limiting judgments and the importance of cultivating an open mind. Eight weeks after my class with Michael, I received a phone call from the client sponsor, with whom just 2 months ago I had shared my perspective about Michael. The sponsor told me he thought it was important I heard the rest of Michael's story. He explained to me that, at the end of the 10-week program, there was a graduation ceremony and one of the program participants was elected by the group to speak at their graduation event. Michael was chosen by his group. In his speech, Michael apparently spoke about his journey of growth.

He spoke of his disagreement with "that guy who taught us Emotional Intelligence" and of his "disregard for the content". He went on to talk about going home and sharing his thoughts with his wife. When she wanted to know more about Emotional Intelligence, he noticed feelings of anger and frustration at her inquiry; yet, he also noticed, perhaps for the first time, he had access to another choice at that moment. Rather than shutting down and walking away from his wife in anger, he took a breath instead, sat down, and asked her to share more. He listened. And, although he felt awkward, he began talking more openly to her about his feelings. Michael continued sharing with the entire group that, over the course of the 10-week program he could see that he was listening more to his colleagues and not acting out from his own emotional reactions. His colleagues nodded in agreement, having clearly witnessed Michael's transformation. While Michael certainly had his doubts and judgments at the beginning, he eventually found wisdom on his own terms.

> "*How do we begin to cultivate an open mind? We must become aware of what we're thinking and feeling. If we can do that, we can continue taking in new information and allow our judgments to evolve.*"

As the client sponsor described all this, I found myself moved to tears. At first, I was ashamed of how judgmental I had been. Yet ultimately, I felt deeply grateful and appreciative that I was being gifted this final story about Michael. My unwillingness to see and suspend those limiting beliefs about Michael's ability (and my own) came at a heavy price. But, in the end, my experience with Michael showed me the power and impact of cultivating an open mind.

Your Rumble Zone

It is typical to see new participants in a drum circle, or other types of musical group experience, very hesitant about joining in. ==Many people do not have an open mind about their ability to hold a beat.== Over and over, I hear, "I'm not musical", or "I don't have rhythm". This self-judgment is coming from some combination of many sources: a former teacher in elementary school who criticized you because you couldn't learn music the "right" way; lack of opportunity to explore your own musical preferences; previous experiences making music with others being less than successful. All these past experiences contribute to the lack of an open mind about one's musical abilities.

And for every judgmental participant, I encounter 3 new drummers who bring an open mind to their first drum circle. Regardless of their past experiences, these new drummers bring an attitude of curiosity stronger than the judgmental voices from their past. Cultivating an open mind requires us to recognize the limiting judgments we hold, reframe them into possibilities, and then continue to push ourselves beyond our comfort zone of the known to the uncomfortable place of the unknown.

Reflections

Review the rumbles in your Rumble Zone where you have limiting judgments about yourself or others involved in the situation. Give yourself permission to explore the "cannots", "won'ts", "will nevers" and "couldn't possibly's". Then, for each limiting judgment, write out your case for the judgment.

- What evidence do you have that the judgment is true?
- Is this evidence fact or assumption?
- When did you make this judgment?
- Do those circumstances still exist? What has changed?

This exploration of the factual side of your judgments offers your logical, conscious brain an opportunity to make its case.

Our limiting judgments are often rooted in emotion, as well as thought. Next, for each limiting judgment, reflect upon your feelings toward yourself and others involved.

- Are your limiting judgments rooted in frustration, anger, resentment, pride, self-righteousness or other emotions that hinder an open mind? These emotions are real. Until you are aware of them and accept them as yours (or others'), they will continue to be a block to your open mind.
- What do you need to do to help transform these emotions? Make contact with the others? Have a conversation?

The opportunity here is to find the willingness to suspend your current judgments, manage your own emotions, and courageously bring an open mind.

Chapter 8

Take Action

> We do not need, and indeed never will have,
> all the answers before we act...
> It is often through taking action that we
> can discover some of them.
>
> –Charlotte Bunch

Each of the strategies to thrive in the rough and tumble of change has one essential element in common. At some point in one's exploration of any of the strategies, there is a moment the rumble calls you to take action. Be it sharing your point of view or asking a question, showing empathy or suspending judgment, awareness may not be enough. To thrive in the rumble, we must take action. And not just action for busyness sake, but action that purposefully moves us closer to where we want to be. Taking action to change limiting beliefs or behavior patterns that have prevented our forward movement. Without taking action, one becomes stuck in the rumble, only halfway to success, and eventually falling back into old habits.

There is relief and reassurance when taking action. Navigating the rumble state is a highly internal process: awareness of yourself and your surroundings; noticing your thoughts and emotions; reflection on the patterns that hold back change; cultivating courage. When we take action in the rumble state, we're moving from the inner world to the outer world. One notices their desire for a career change and, despite their fear, attends a class to learn a new skill. One puts off a difficult conversation with a colleague for fear that he won't listen, and now the meeting has been scheduled. One does what one's been asked to do because, regardless of their challenges with the organization, they've been hired to do a job. When we take action, we're manifesting the next reality that will be co-created around us. We're doing our part within a dynamic, multi-connected ecosystem of change.

If we are intentional in the rumble, we can live a life moving towards our personal and professional dreams.

Being in the rumble space is a time of ambiguity which often triggers fear or confusion. In this in-between state, where the new hasn't emerged yet, taking a purposeful action can provide a moment of solace in the storm. That's exactly what happened to me when I was diagnosed with cancer.

A New Mindset

It was my second trip to the hospital for a biopsy. Just five days ago, I noticed a lump in my neck. I told my naturopathic doctor about it. He leaped quickly into action. Although he subscribes to the approach of using natural remedies, nutrition, and life-style change to help the body heal, he also believes western medicine is necessary when facing a potential disease. Alarmed at the lump, he had ordered a biopsy.

I brought a friend with me for support to the first biopsy. I really didn't know what to expect. I felt fine, certain it wasn't cancer. When I got the call from the hospital reporting the lump as benign, I was thrilled.

But my naturopath wasn't. When he called me, having received the same results, there was concern in his voice. He explained he had ordered a fine needle, ultrasound-guided biopsy to get an exact location under the lump. The pathologist who did the biopsy didn't use the ultrasound. My naturopath wasn't convinced the extracted sample tested the lump properly, so he asked me to go back the next day for another biopsy. Not wanting to burden a friend with another trip to the hospital for what I was sure would be another false alarm, I went alone.

The pathologist was quite snippy towards my naturopath's opinion, not trusting a doctor who didn't go to traditional medical school. Nonetheless, he performed the second biopsy. And when he came back with the new results, the look on his face instantly initiated a rumble in me before he even spoke a word.

"It's a good thing you came back," he began. "The lump is a malignant cancer on your thyroid. We'll need to do additional testing to determine the exact type and stage of your cancer."

And there it is. New external information shattering my pattern of beliefs that my body is invincible. But it's no surprise that these are my beliefs. After all, I'm 36 years old and never had a disease in my life. I don't know anyone my age who has cancer. It isn't part of the framework of my life. Yet suddenly it is. Welcome to the beginning of a rumble. Fear, anxiety, overwhelm, and despair are the ruling emotions. New pathways and new possibilities are far beyond my comprehension.

> "*When we take action, we're doing our part within a dynamic, multi-connected ecosystem of change.*"

As I drive back home, I'm overcome with everything I need to do. A longer-term care plan is called for. Call the doctor. Schedule lab work. Find an endocrinologist. Tell my family. But in the midst of all that, I remember there's a short-term plan already in place that I have to deal with. Tomorrow, I'm scheduled to get on a plane to San Francisco and meet with Arthur Hull, my teacher of drum circle facilitation, to collaborate with him on a mentor program that we are going to teach in a few months. How is all that going to happen now?

I arrived home to an empty house and started making calls to family and friends. We're all now stumbling into our own version of the rumble this diagnosis is initiating. I'm flooded with questions and emotions. There's lots of ambiguity; yet only one clear next step. Go meet Arthur Hull.

Getting on a plane, focusing on a task, and fulfilling a commitment is a good set of actions to take. I feel useful. I'm doing something outside of myself that will contribute to others in the long run. I'm eager to partner with Arthur to create this program. While I'm excited driving up to his house, I'm also settling into another dose of reality about my cancer.

Arthur greets me with a hug. "I've got good news and bad news," I begin. Then I tell him what happened. His expression shifts from happiness to confusion and shock. "What can I do to help?" he asks. Without hesitation, I reply, "Let's get to work."

Empowered through Action

There is a power, an empowerment, that can result from taking action. It creates energy. The action of designing the mentor program didn't heal my illness or change the diagnosis. It didn't create the new pathway from the rumble. The rumble I was in would be a long one, stretching from diagnosis to surgery to radiation. I would incorporate many of these strategies to ultimately thrive in the rumble of cancer. But now, to be able to take action and focus on a larger purpose was the best medicine my spirit needed to navigate this sudden, massive change.

As a learning and development professional, my commitment is to help people find the greatest leverage point to their own success – themselves. They must be willing to reflect on their experiences and look for ways to improve themselves by learning something new. Yet, learning is not the last step of the development process. We have to figure out how to bring this learning into real, grounded action. In fact, that's the complaint of many training efforts. "This is all interesting, but what am I supposed to do differently?"

Navigating change, showing individual leadership, and learning something new often involve actions in three areas:

- Adopting a new mindset or attitude
- Having a conversation with another person
- Accomplishing an individual "to do"

In the rumble, taking action serves to move change forward. Through your actions, you empower yourself as well as others. You increase confidence in the ability to meet the goal. And you balance the inner reflections necessary to rumble.

In the chapter, Bring an Open Mind, we looked at strategies and ideas that help shift our mindset. When we work with our own judgmentalism, we're taking an action that, over time, impacts our attitudes and mindsets. In Strive for Empathy, we discussed the action of showing compassion to another amid a change you're making. But, sometimes, taking an action may get us more deeply mired; increase our confusion or insecurity. If that happens, if we are stuck in the rumble looking for all kinds of excuses and reasons to avoid taking action, we may need a little help from the outside. We may need a conversation with a friend.

Follow the Signs

I'm 5 miles from the state line between Texas and Oklahoma. My moving van just got a flat tire and the rental company is sending a tow truck to fix it. It won't get here for another ninety minutes. So I'm stuck on the side of the highway waiting. Questions and doubts race through my head. Why am I leaving Texas? What am I going to do in Seattle? Am I making the biggest mistake of my life? I convince myself that the answer is obvious. This flat tire at the state line is surely a sign from God that I should turn around and go back. What on earth was I thinking? I quit my job in Texas as a Director of a software company. I have no job prospects in Seattle. I'm someone who always has a plan – I would never ever do something crazy like this. My background has been exclusively in engineering and technology. And now I'm going to be a drum circle facilitator? Join a group of drummers in Seattle, people I hardly know, who I met on my trip to Hawaii? No wonder my sister thinks I've joined a cult!

Of course, there's a deeper part of me that knows, somehow, this is what I need to do, despite how insane it seems. I know I'm listening to a wisdom that goes beyond any logic. Yet the anxiety, uncertainty, and self-doubt still continue to plague me. Every inner voice shouts that I'm making a huge mistake. That I should run back to Dallas. That this flat tire is a clear, indisputable, undeniable sign from the universe to go home. I'm barely holding it together when the tow truck pulls up behind my van. An ordinary blue pickup truck. I can't see the driver, but to me he represents a knight in shining armor. He'll fix the flat and then I'll turn right around and drive back to Dallas. I'm smart enough to not ignore this sign and last-minute chance for redemption. I'll return to Texas, unload the truck, and figure out the rest later. It will be humiliating, but at least I did the right thing.

"In the rumble, taking action serves to move change forward. You empower yourself as well as others."

The driver of the tow truck is older than I imagine, probably in his sixties, an African American man with gray hair and a bit of gray stubble for a beard. He's dressed in a pair of old denim overalls. We shake hands. He looks over at the moving van, looks back at me, and tells me fixing the tire will be no problem at all. Then, he asks me a simple question; a question that amplifies all those voices still screaming in my head. "Where are you moving?"

That was all I needed. A dam bursts and before I know it, I'm crying and spilling my life to this total stranger. Telling him everything. How I discovered the drumming in Hawaii, how much it changed me, my fears about leaving Texas, my struggle with my own sexuality. In tears, I end the story with my conviction that the flat tire is surely a sign from God to give up and go home. The driver is leaning on the van, hand on his hip in a stance that feels somehow comforting and familiar. His stance alone tells me it's all going to be okay. "Son, let me tell you a story," he begins. He speaks slowly, his voice deep and relaxed. He starts to describe how twenty years ago he was a high school math teacher. He and his wife had two children. He was putting food on the table with that teaching job. "But my heart wasn't in it," he says. "I like to fix things, work with my hands." Yet, despite knowing that, he continued to teach because he thought it was the right thing for himself and his family. As the years passed, he became unhappy and resentful that he was spending so much time doing something he didn't love. "So one day," he goes on, "I quit my job and tell my wife that I'm going to open my own business. I bought this truck and started doing what was important to me." He pulls out a cloth to wipe his brow. "Now I've got 6 of these trucks," he goes on, proudly, "more than a dozen employees, and me and my family are happier than ever. All because I followed my dream." He sticks the cloth in his back pocket. "So, I'm going to get to work here. I'm going to change this tire and get this van on the road so you can follow your dream. You may not know exactly what's ahead of you, but you know the right direction. Let me fix this tire so you can get going."

He was true to his word. The tire was fixed in no time. I thanked him, got back in the van and, without any more hesitation whatsoever, I headed straight for Seattle. If I was looking for a sign straight from heaven, he had just appeared as an angel in a tow truck wearing denim overalls.

Asking for or getting support when you're taking action is nothing to be ashamed of. Sometimes it's absolutely necessary. Yet taking an action step doesn't mean the Rumble is over. It's not necessarily the last step that happens on the new pathway. The action may lead you to another limiting pattern that needs to be broken or another need to rally courage. But you won't know what's next until you take action where you are. Meaningful, potent action. To thrive in the rumble and emerge wiser, more in sync with your surroundings, and more deeply connected to yourself and others, you will have to, whether it's easy or difficult, take that next step.

Your Rumble Zone

1, 2, let's all play. Every drum circle facilitator trained by Arthur Hull knows this phrase as the Call to Groove. It's the drum circle facilitator's invitation for every drummer to contribute their unique rhythmic pattern to our shared groove. In response to this invitation, we go from silence to drumbeats, called to immediate action.

Another phrase a drum circle facilitator can use to invite drummers to play is "at your leisure…". The intention with this phrase is for each drummer to listen to their surroundings, consider their options and join the song when it's right for them, not in response to a directive. Both calls inspire action, and both remind me of what is required to take action in the rough and tumble of change.

Sometimes in the midst of a new or challenging situation in life, as in response to the call to groove, our actions are changes in behaviors. We learn a new skill. We do something different. Other times, we need to assess the situation and consider when is the best time to take action. There is a fine but important line between waiting for the right time and procrastinating over a dreaded task. How do you make that distinction?

Reflections

Taking action in response to a rumble in life often falls into three categories

1. Behavior Change – incorporating a new or different skill in a task or in relating to others

2. Attitude Adjustment – awareness of one's current emotional state and its impact on others, then choosing a different attitude

3. Mindset Shift – willingness to consider other people's points of view as valid

Consider these questions to identify the possible actions you can take.

- Which of your rumbles is calling you to take some form of action?

- What simple action(s) can you take right now?

- What behavior patterns are holding you back from fully engaging in the rumble?

- What behavior changes could you adopt to break through a current hurdle you are facing?

- Can you change your attitude by reaching out to others?

- What core beliefs do you hold that are out of sync with your reality today?

- How can you shift your mindset to accept that your core beliefs are changing?

Chapter 9

Find Resilience

> My scars remind me that I did indeed survive
> my deepest wounds...they remind me that the damage
> life has inflicted on me has, in many places, left me
> stronger and more resilient. What hurt me in the past
> has actually made me better equipped to face
> the present.
>
> –Steve Goodier

The scene is a tent large enough for a 2-ring circus, with concentric circles of chairs emanating from a small circle in the middle of the tent. Surrounding the tent are RVs and smaller tents housing the hundreds of would-be drummers, all there to support this marathon drumming spectacular. They were there for the drumming, the community, the fun, and most importantly, their commitment to beating cancer. The event was put on by DRUMSTRONG, an organization run by a drum circle facilitator, Scott Swimmer. After successfully supporting his son's battle against childhood cancer, Scott committed himself to raising money and awareness to help others beat cancer. DRUMSTRONG is now a world-wide series of drum circle events, all raising money for the local community's battle against cancer. The central heartbeat of DRUMSTRONG is the annual 24-hour drumming marathon in North Carolina.

This was the 5th year of this event, and to create additional excitement and money, each year an hour was added to the length of the marathon. This was a 29-hour drum circle, but right now the clock mounted above the tent logging the minutes read 20 hours. It was 4:30 a.m. and we had 9 hours to go.

The peak participation of the drum circle, so far, was about 7 hours ago. There were hundreds under the tent, but there were still more seats waiting to be filled. The music had ranged from a loud cacophony of drummers learning to play together to a connected group creating and riding their own rhythmic waves. Each hour, a new facilitator would step in to help the group navigate transitions and continue the groove. Part of the marathon is the commitment to keep a continuous beat of some kind going for 29 hours.

Music is powerful medicine for the body and the spirit. This is one of the primary drivers for the increased demand for drum circle facilitators around the country, and the world. The drum is a musical instrument that has a very low barrier of entry to play. Never played a musical instrument before? That's ok. You have limited mobility? We have instruments to accommodate many needs. With drummers ready to play, the facilitators help bring out the best rhythmic music the group can make. This approach gives everyone not only the ability to hear the rhythmical groove (which promotes healing) but also play with an ensemble (which promotes healing exponentially). Hospitals, assisted living facilities, and hospice care all have found the power of group music in creating moments of peace and happiness.

I hadn't planned on coming to DRUMSTRONG or facilitating, but I wanted to get away. So, at the last minute, I changed plans and found myself in North Carolina.

I knew many of the professionals scheduled to facilitate DRUMSTRONG and was welcomed to the event and to the facilitation team. There were only a limited number of spots left open on the schedule. I picked 4:30AM. The facilitator before me had carried the group through the late-night hours in years past. The person who was to facilitate at sunrise was also set. But there was a spot in between those 2 that was yet to be assigned. In fact, they thought they may have to each extend their time to cover the slot. My arrival proved to be the final puzzle piece in the DRUMSTRONG schedule.

I played as a member of the circle off and on during the hours leading up to my facilitation at 4:30 AM. I took breaks, talked with friends, and felt I had made the best decision in coming to the event. I was playing again when the circle was at its peak. My mind began to wander as

I played. I took myself out of the moment. I began to think about my facilitation at 4:30 AM. I began to dread it. The peak groove was so much fun. The energy in the circle was electric with hundreds of drums, bells, shakers and woodblocks playing an improvisational orchestration. While playing my own drum as part of this groove, I began to create a story about what it would be like at 4:30 AM: small group, low energy, sleepy people. How was I going to make that work and match what was happening at the peak? I began to plan my defeat before I had even started. Sometimes, resilience is required, not to overcome an actual defeat, but the story of defeat we create in our head.

> *"Resilience is our capacity to recover quickly from difficulties - the choice towards optimism and belief in possibility."*

The facilitator leading the circle called for a full group stop of the music. We went from hundreds of sounds to silence in a count of 4. That broke me out of the story of defeat spinning in my head and brought me back to the current moment of the drum circle. I saw friends and strangers with smiles on their faces. I saw Scott embrace his son, reminding me why I was here in the first place. That jolt back to the present moment jolted me out of my dread for my circle, and back to the reason I chose to come to DRUMSTRONG. I was here because I needed rejuvenation from my community. And I was here because I believe in the power of the drum circle. And this event in particular, raising money to beat cancer, was near and dear to my heart. There was no room for dread here. My spirit had received a boost from the jolt. This boost in spirit and reminder of purpose lit the fuse of my resilience.

Resilience is our capacity to recover quickly from difficulties. Others may see the hurdle as impossible to overcome, but resilience is the choice towards optimism in the moment and belief in possibility, again.

I have seen the resilience of an elder finding the strength to continue to live on his own. The person suffering from chronic depression, finding the resilience to break through the silence and share her pain in an effort to help others. The manager who has a series of difficult conversations at work on the same day their spouse has asked for a divorce.

When we tap into our resilience, we are calling upon our physical, emotional and spiritual self. The more we strengthen these internal human systems within us, the more able we are to choose resilience in the face of an expected or unexpected rumble.

In other words, resilience is about caring for ourselves on every level. Our physical bodies have to be able to get up, move around, take action, engage people in conversation. But if we're not feeling well, we're less likely to have the ability to do those things. For the emotional self, it's about acknowledging and attending to what we're feeling. It's not about making the emotion go away or denying it. Sometimes you just have to sit with the discomfort. As we sit with the emotion, we develop the muscle to choose resilience again and again. The spiritual is what calls us outside of ourselves. It helps us connect to an idea greater than ourselves. And, in times of upheaval and stress, where no hope seems to exist, it is in spirit that you can find the strength to go on.

I had temporarily overcome the story of defeat I created in my head about the circle at 4:30 AM. But having the resilience to continue to overcome my made-up stories will need more than a boost in my spirit. Resilience also requires that I can physically endure the challenge. I need enough sleep to be at my best. When I arrived at DRUMSTRONG, I was already physically exhausted. Weeks on the road, teaching workshops, and other family obligations had left little time for rest. I had been running on fumes and adrenaline. The answer was obvious, but for me, the choice was difficult. Take a nap: I didn't need to stay up continuously until 4:30 AM. It was 11 PM. I had been offered a place to nap in an RV. But again, my story kicked in: A real, tough, committed, good facilitator would suck it up, stay up, and be present with the circle the entire time. Again, I created a story that brought me down. I was having this conversation with myself outside of the drumming tent, and I could hear the rhythms as the story spun in my head. And like before, the facilitator called for a break in the music. The jolt of full groove to silence once again brought me to being present. Suddenly I could see that I was being ridiculous. Take a nap. Accept the offer. I chose to physically recharge. It was clear that my spirit alone could not offer all I would need to overcome my mindset and step into the facilitator role. I needed the physical strength and stamina to give the energy needed to lead a group of drummers and keep the energy going at 4:30 AM. And to do that, I needed to care for my physical self.

I woke up at 4:00 AM feeling much stronger. The groove in the circle was a quiet, steady presence created by nine men and women, all giving themselves fully to the collective song. I entered the circle, made eye contact with the previous facilitator, and joined the existing groove. Although I feel rested from my nap, anxiety about taking over starts causing my foot to tap much faster than the current beat– that's not good.

We continue to play, and the transition from the previous facilitator to me is seamless. No words are needed by either of us. He stands, points in my direction and leaves the circle. Everyone knows what's happening. My foot still tapping too fast, my hands playing lightly on my drum, I focus on my breath. I look at the peaceful faces of the men and women in the circle, all with eyes closed. I hear the continuous, rhythmical groove. And yet, I still feel nervous. To be here, in this role of facilitator, I'll have to learn how to be aware of my anxiety and yet at the same time, allow the musical magic that is happening to continue. My biggest job is not to get in the way. Resilience is needed to endure the continuous rush of fear while staying engaged in the circle. Sitting with an uncomfortable emotion as another component of resilience became a source of strength for me. I found the resilience to keep the beat alive by not getting in the way of it. The beat goes on, like life. It's our job to believe in the possibility and tap into resilience when times are tough.

At the end of my hour, as I made eye contact with the next facilitator, I felt a sense of peace. As I walked away from the circle, the sun was just about to rise. The sky was a beautiful soft blue. I had arrived at DRUMSTRONG totally exhausted, but now I felt alive. Just like the sun which keeps rising day after day, I just need to keep showing up and choosing resilience.

The Power of Optimism

Some of the first scientific research proving the positive impact of group drumming on individual wellness used healthcare workers as the study population. Caregivers know resilience. Caregivers, whether paid professionals or family members, often face situations requiring resilience to continue their efforts in the face of insurmountable challenges. Caregivers who work with patients nearing end of life have a particular challenge when called upon to be optimistic. The resilience they tap into is not in support of accomplishing a long-term goal. This is resilience to care for another, right now, in the face of their certain death. That's one of the keys to tapping into resilience. The recognition that, no matter the challenge, we can still make a life-affirming choice.

I had been the recipient of that depth of care from friends and family during my battle with cancer. I had firsthand experience of watching someone go the extra mile to care for me, on top of all their own commitments in life. I've also been a caregiver. I know the resilience I had to tap into to patiently listen to my mother repeat the same questions over and over again as her mind failed in dementia. I love her. I'm frustrated. I am heart broken. How can I feel all these emotions at the same time? I had to sit with all the emotions and resiliently continue to be with her.

As DRUMSTRONG approached its 28th hour, a plan emerged for the closing hour. Any of the facilitators who led throughout the marathon would make a return for a final set in the last hour. I was tired and exhilarated. I had tapped into the resilience to make it through the night and through my early morning facilitation. As my time in the final circle approached, I was brought back to the circle I facilitated before sunrise. I remembered the women and men who were caretaking the rhythm to ensure it continued, all the while knowing it would eventually end.

"The rumble will test you to the edge of your limits."

Throughout the DRUMSTRONG 29-hour marathon, there were stories and tributes of those who battled cancer and were benefiting from the efforts of DRUMSTRONG. Their voice was strong in the event. Their resilience to continue in the face of their challenges was inspiring. So, in the final circle, I asked everyone who was a cancer survivor to continue to play while everyone else stopped. This was the cancer survivor's rhythmic song. I then invited any caregivers to stand. I dedicated this cancer survivor's song not to the survivors, but to the caregivers. I thanked them for caring for each of us as we navigated the unexpected journey of cancer. It was their resilience that helped us to be alive today. Their resilience fueled our recovery and our life.

The Seed of Choice

Imagine a single dandelion flower growing out of a small crack in the concrete slab of a parking lot. There are no other plants, flowers or grass growing anywhere in sight. There is only this single flower. What does it take for that small seed, dropped on the soil maybe before the parking lot was created, to go from underneath all that concrete to emerge into the sunlight for nourishment and life? It had to wait for the right circumstances and follow its innate drive to sprout and live. It didn't have to manage a preconceived judgment that it couldn't survive. Instinct drove the seed to flourish. Once it had the resources required, it didn't have a choice but to respond to the call of life.

The rumble will test you to the edge of your limits. You want to get from where you are to where you want to be – there is an inner calling to learn, adapt and connect. You will encounter boundaries that will test your limits. How much ambiguity can you bear? How much ego will have to die? But, unlike the flower, which has no choice but to answer the call of life - we can choose. We must choose. Sometimes we don't recognize our choices as choices. We say we "have to" do this or we "can't" do that. And, almost always, those "haves" and "can'ts" represent our own self-limiting and self-doubting choice. A choice away from the call of life.

To choose resilience in the rumble, we need the right circumstances and resources, just like the flower. The seed waits resiliently in the cold, dark ground for the time when its instinct will take over. We, however, can't rely on instinct alone to answer the call from life. We have a choice. I chose when to come out as a gay man. I chose all those times when I did not come out because I didn't believe others would accept me. I could have chosen to drive back to Dallas after the moving truck had the flat tire, but I made a different choice and continued to Seattle. I didn't choose to have cancer, but I did choose my response to the disease. I fought, I learned, and I asked for help – these were all choices I made.

Within all those larger choices are the small choices I make every day to live my life in the middle of those rumbles. Choosing to live my life openly as a gay man was a single choice, but the act of choosing to acknowledge who I am is a choice I encounter over and over. In front of a class, meeting a new colleague, holding hands with my partner in the movie theater. All those are everyday choices I make in the moment to support my larger choice of living openly. Sometimes I am conscious of the choice, and sometimes I am not. Sometimes I make the choice a thousand times before it feels natural. Sometimes I'm so sick and tired of making the choice that I falter, only to return to the point of knowing I will need to make a choice again. Rarely do I make a choice only once and it works out well and I feel good and solid about the choice. Resilience in the rumble is having the patience to wait for the right time to emerge; gathering the resources needed to make the choice; and making the choice towards life – and choosing it again and again and again…

There is no magic bullet to thriving in the rumble. There's no magic wand I can wave to help you see the patterns that need breaking or identify the strategy that will set the best intention for you. I can provide frameworks, questions, strategies and stories to show that it has been done and it can be done again. Sometimes it looks like magic when you see others change and grow. Sometimes, it feels like magic when you are in the moment of clarity, of joy, of hope as you see the new pathway emerging. But it's not magic; it's individual choice – it's leadership. And with that new pathway comes the inevitable next rumble moment. And with it, your opportunity to choose and choose and choose again.

Your Rumble Zone

Boom BOOM. Boom BOOM. Listen closely. Can you hear your heartbeat? Can you feel it beating as it pushes the blood through your veins? ==The heartbeat is the beat we all have in common.== The beat we all have access to. In the drum circle, the heartbeat rhythm is a grounding rhythm. It's a rhythm that reminds us of life, of the continual persistence life has in calling us into growth, into connection, into the rumble.

When we prepare physically, emotionally, and spiritually to be resilient in the face of change, we are tapping into the same life force the heartbeat represents. The enduring passion that comes from a sense of purpose. The physical prowess we hear in a strong heartbeat. The emotional strength displayed when accepting the emotion at hand.

Reflections

Tapping into the well of resilience is a choice towards the heartbeat – it's a choice for life. Just as the groove in the drum circle uses the lowest-sounding note as an organizing beacon, we all have a common frame of reference for life – the heartbeat. When we choose resilience, we choose to align with this powerful and universal life force. And while we share this common pulse, we are also unique in our expression of it. We have an opportunity to take the next step, to endure the rough and tumble, and continue our effort to get where we want to be.

- What do you need to do to strengthen your resilience to continue your efforts in the changes in your life?

- How can you best care for your physical self to be able to offer your strongest effort?

- What emotions feel the hardest to accept, or at least acknowledge?

- How can you feel the emotion but not react? How can you endure the feeling and know it too will pass?

- How does your overall purpose motivate you in this change?

- What greater good are you supporting as you decide, once again, to make the effort to move forward on a new path, even when it feels impossible?

Resilience means you are willing, in your own unique way, to do what it takes, to let your heartbeat rise above the doubt and fear, and be present in the rumble.

Chapter 10

Navigating the Rumble of the Moment

As this book goes to publication in June of 2020, the world is in the midst of what is more than likely the Rumble of my lifetime, the Covid-19 pandemic. The rough and tumble of change has been imposed on all of us. Uncertainty lies in every direction: Will I get sick? Are my loved ones going to suffer? Who do I know personally who will die? How will those less privileged economically pay their rent and feed their families? How will our society respond?

We are being plunged into this not by choice. It's here. Our choices lie in how we navigate this Rumble Zone.

How do we, as individuals and as a community, care for ourselves and others in this time in between what was and what is emerging?

I cannot answer that question for everyone. I can only answer for me, in this moment. And, like the tech company using their own software to solve their own problem, or the musician who seeks solace in the creative process, I turn to my own work to find understanding and direction. **If I don't start with my own beliefs, why do I hold them in the first place?**

For you, the reader, I hope these closing words give you a road map to use these leadership strategies in your own Rumble Zone. For me, I hope these words nurture my own resilience for myself, my family and all our communities.

Applying the Rumble Strategies

The strategies explored in this book are not used in isolation, as single step-by-step procedures. They are all at play at once, each contributing to your overall efforts in dealing with change. This happens on an unconscious level. Humans are made to adapt. But sometimes, our ability to adapt is challenged; we become stuck in self-judgment, doubt or fear. We lose touch with our beliefs. We feel lost. And, we may not even realize that is happening. Instead, we just think we need to try harder or blame others. It's at this point, when our natural ability to navigate tough times falters, when we must stop. Stop the doing. Stop the trying. Stop the self-judgment.

For the past month, I've struggled to stop. As the impact of the pandemic has exponentially exploded around the world, I've done almost anything but really stopped.

- I've blamed myself for being part of the problem: I travel the world, hopping on and off planes without giving real thought to my contribution to spreading local viruses globally.

- I've distracted myself with media, news and entertainment. But those distractions take me out of the moment of my situation and lead me to worries of a future that is unwritten.

- I've self-medicated myself with food and alcohol. Those give me comfort in the moment, but a false comfort of immediate pleasure that is actually doing more harm than good to my own immune system.

So today, I stopped. I took a breath. And I looked at the diagram below. This picture lays out all the rumble strategies and reminds me of their interconnectedness to my rumble zone.

Intentionally and consciously navigating the rumble of the moment does have a starting place: I must **be present** to the situation and my current thoughts and feelings. It may take personal **courage** to stop doing and start feeling. It can be scary to feel emotion.

But feeling our emotion and attending to that part of our biology strengthens our **resilience**. In the time of change, resilience is called upon as never before. Resilience helps us **take action** in the most challenging times; not action for distraction, but actions of service, of kindness and of creativity.

In times of change, we may need to learn new ways of doing things. To learn new ways of doing things, we need to bring an open mind. Our ingrained patterns may not serve this new situation. Our open minds allow for true curiosity to learn how we can adapt and how others are adapting.

As we engage with others, I want to remember to bring empathy for others, who are also having their own thoughts and feelings in response to the disruptive change. As I gather new information from others and new ideas from my creativity, I arrive at a deeper understanding of my current point of view, my current thoughts. And if I'm continually mindful of myself, I'm hearing those thoughts, feeling my feelings, and again aware of my true state.

I realized my path to navigate this rumble starts now with **being present** to my current thoughts and feelings. Right now, I feel sad and scared. I have negative, self-judgmental thoughts. Acknowledging my feelings doesn't make them go away or fix the situation. It does, however, name my true state. It gives voice to that part of my brain that does not consciously choose emotion but needs to be acknowledged before other parts of my brain can be fully engaged.

After I was present to my thoughts and feelings, I pulled out my journal and wrote the following: *I'm feeling sad and scared. But that's not doing anyone else any good, and I want to help others. I'm not a doctor or a nurse, so what can I do? I can use my own expertise and do what I do in a relevant way – and do it as best I can in this challenge. I can share The Rumble Zone strategies I'm using now, to help me make sense of this pandemic.*

Using this process, for me, is more than an academic thought exercise. It's a practice full of insight, awareness, and actions that have helped me get through this pandemic.

- **Being present** to my emotions allowed me to feel my sadness and my fear.

- Awareness of my own sadness and fear allowed me to have **empathy** for the sadness and fear others may be feeling.

- Empathy for the emotions of others reminded me of my **point of view regarding** the importance of service.

- I can be of service by providing my point of view to others, which led me to take the **action** of writing these closing words.

- As I near the end of these closing words, I feel relief and **resilience** for knowing I'm doing my small part to contribute to the greater good.

- Feeling relief allows me to breathe, to see the beauty of the day as the daffodils bloom in the garden and as the sun shines on my face.

Is this state of relief permanent? Of course not. The global pandemic is not resolved because of my small contribution. But, if I focus on the immensity of it all, I'm not present to my surroundings and my current feelings. So, I try again to just be present to what is around me. And I choose to come back to myself – again and again and again.

I believe this practice helps me navigate the rumble of this moment. The actions will change. The feelings will shift wildly. The challenge of being empathic will be harder with some people than others. But the heartbeat of those of us alive today still beats. And if the heartbeat is there, the willingness to look deeply and honestly at myself is not far behind.

> May we all navigate this and every rumble with
> awareness, compassion, courage, and most of all, hope.

Review Inquiry

Hi, it's Jim Boneau.

I hope you've enjoyed the book, finding it both useful and inspirational. How about helping spread the word about rumble? If you are open, I have a favor to ask you.

Would you consider giving it a rating on Amazon or wherever you bought the book? Online book stores are more likely to promote a book when they feel good about its content, and reader reviews are a great barometer for a book's quality. And, given the 2 different topics featured in the book, drumming and corporate leadership development, endorsements help groups from one world reach out to another… and vise versa.

So, please go to Amazon.com (or wherever you bought the book), search for my name and the book title, and leave a review. If someone gave you a copy of my book, then leave a review on Amazon, and maybe consider adding a picture of you holding the book or even playing a drum. That increases the likelihood your review will be accepted!

In addition, if you are inspired to try a drum circle, please write to me and tell me your experience. I love to hear everyone's first drum circle experience story.

Many thanks in advance,

Jim Boneau

Will You Share the Love and Share the Rumble?

Get this book for a friend, associate or family member!

If you have found this book valuable and know others who would find it useful, consider buying them a copy as a gift. Special bulk discounts are available if you would like your whole team or organization to benefit from reading this.

Just contact

jim@therumblegroup.com
or visit
therumblezone.com.

Would You Like Jim Boneau to Speak to Your Organization?

Book Jim Now!

Jim accepts a limited number of speaking/coaching/training engagements each year. To learn how you can bring his message to your organization, email jim@therumblegroup.com. Look for links to his videos at therumblezone.com.

This photo is Jim leading the closing ceremony at the World Parkinson's Congress in Portland, OR, USA in 2017. Jim was honored to be invited to lead the event by Judi Spencer.

Resources

Find additional resources to help you lead and learn at **www.therumblezone.com/resources.**

For more on Arthur Hull, Village Music Circles, and the world wide Drum Circle Facilitation movement, visit **www.drumcircle.com**.

To find a certified Village Music Circles Global Trainer in your part of the world, visit **https://www.villagemusiccirclesglobal.com/**. It was my honor to help certify each of these individuals to be Global Trainers for VMC, using the curriculum I created with Arthur.

There are other teachers for drum circle facilitation beyond Village Music Circles. To find a locally trained drum circle facilitator in your area, visit the Drum Circle Facilitators Guild (**dcfg.net**). The Guild is an organization committed to promoting health, wellness, and fun through community building, led by qualified facilitators.

To learn more about therapeutic uses for rhythm, visit **www.healthrhythms.com/** and **Rhythm2Recovery.com**.

To learn more about local artisans around the world and how to bring their instruments to your area, look for music retailers offering products from JAMTOWN, a Fair Trade certified importer.

To see the application of drum circles into the broader field of Music Therapy, visit **ubdrumcircles.com/** and the work of Christine Stevens.

To learn how to create a business as a drum circle facilitator, visit **marytolena.com/**.

To help beat cancer, visit **drumstrong.org/**.

Visit **remo.com** to purchase manufactured hand drums to start your own community drum circle. Also, find Remo endorsed drum circle facilitators at **https://remo.com/team/recreation/**.

In your own local community, go to your local musical instrument store and ask about local drumming artists and other resources.

If you are considering writing a book, my book coach, Marcia Zina Mager is outstanding in helping first time authors write. Her email is **marciazinamager@gmail.com**.

For a publishing partner, look up Ignite Press at **ignitepress.us**.

About the Author

JIM BONEAU is an internationally recognized executive coach and facilitator of leadership and organizational development workshops. Leaders and teams who work with Jim strengthen their ability to effectively communicate strategy, build bonds of trust, and cascade the organization's values and vision with their teams, partners and customers. Jim's approach challenges leaders to renew their individual leadership beliefs and engage in meaningful dialog with their colleagues to turn those beliefs into actions that increase performance and create positive work environments.

Jim has over 25 years working in organizations in a variety of roles: first as a systems engineer, then team and organizational leader, and for the past 15 years as an external coach and facilitator. Jim served as Vice President of Bluepoint Leadership Development before launching his own coaching and facilitation business, The Rumble Group.

As Founder of The Rumble Group, Jim is merging the worlds of traditional leadership development and rhythm to create a new, immersive growth and development methodology. Igniting innovation, accelerating change and creating new pathways for personal and professional development are benefits clients are discovering through Rumble.

Jim has coached and facilitated senior and executive leaders in organizations, including Microsoft, General Electric, Qualcomm, The Mayo Clinic, American Association of Corporate Counsel and Unity Technologies among others. Jim has worked extensively internationally, from coaching executives in a Greek shipping company to recently launching new initiatives in leadership coaching and development in China. Jim was the primary workshop facilitator for multiple faculty groups, teaching and coaching extensively throughout Asia, Europe, and the Americas.

Jim honed his facilitation skills through years of classroom hours teaching Emotional Intelligence, interpersonal relationship skills and other leadership development topics in corporate settings internationally. Jim's expertise as an experiential facilitator has been sharpened by his work as a drum circle facilitator. Jim is a trainer for Village Music Circles, certified to teach the VMC drum circle facilitator workshops. In addition, Jim is the developer and trainer of the VMC Mentor program, building leadership skills for community development. Jim has partnered with Arthur Hull for 20 years, leading workshops around the globe. Jim has led hundreds of large-scale rhythm workshops, inspiring increased innovation, accelerated change and profound insights for personal and organizational leadership. Jim has taught drum circle facilitation skills for over 20 years in the US, Europe and Japan.

Jim's passion for drum circle facilitation shows in his commitment to community drumming in his hometown of Seattle, WA. Jim has served as President of the Seattle World Percussion Society and Chaired the Seattle World Rhythm Festival. For the past 8 years, Jim has been part of the team facilitating 3 days of community rhythm circles at the Northwest Folklife festival, creating opportunities for hundreds of new families to learn about drumming. Jim supports multiple small community circles throughout the year.

In addition to his professional accomplishments, Jim is also committed to community development, both inside organizations and in communities at large. Jim has used his skills to lead city-wide diversity conversations in Seattle, offer community development experiences for immigrant families and lead events for a variety of non-profit organizations. Community, relationships and nurturing potential are at the heart of all Jim's work.

Jim has a master's degree in Applied Behavioral Science from the Leadership Institute of Seattle and is a certified coach through the Hudson Institute. Jim's presence is engaging and direct; and yet he knows the work is not about him, but about the leaders he works with, who then go forward with a renewed sense of passion and purpose for their own leadership goals.

Jim can be reached at: **therumblegroup.com**

Made in the USA
Monee, IL
23 October 2020